FASHODA
THE INCIDENT AND ITS DIPLO-
MATIC SETTING

THE UNIVERSITY OF CHICAGO PRESS
CHICAGO, ILLINOIS

THE BAKER & TAYLOR COMPANY
NEW YORK

THE MACMILLAN COMPANY OF CANADA, LIMITED
TORONTO

THE CAMBRIDGE UNIVERSITY PRESS
LONDON

THE MARUZEN-KABUSHIKI-KAISHA
TOKYO, OSAKA, KYOTO, FUKUOKA, SENDAI

THE COMMERCIAL PRESS, LIMITED
SHANGHAI

TABLE OF CONTENTS

PART I. THE INCIDENT

PART I
THE INCIDENT

CHAPTER I

THE ENCOUNTER AT FASHODA

When the waters of the White Nile escape north-ward from Lake Albert they travel at first between high, well-defined banks and with a good fall and current. But a hundred and fifty miles downstream, and just above Gondokoro, they begin to slacken and presently to lose themselves east and west in vast marshes, through which there run at last only sluggish and much diminished veins of open water. The main stream, however, still drains northward, end-lessly turning and bending through limitless flats of reeds and water-grasses. Eventually, and at about seven degrees of latitude from its source, its thin current drifts feebly through the eastern end of Lake No, which is a long shallow lagoon of dead water surrounded by an immense and dismal labyrinth of pools, islands, and false channels.[1]

Into the western end of the lake is drawn like-wise the slack discharge of another swamp-dissipated river, the Bahr-el-Ghazelle, which brings down to the Nile the collected drainage of the eastern slope of the Nile-Congo watershed. The Bahr-el-Ghazelle heads in the low plateaus of Dar Fertit and the country of the Nyam-Nyams in the far west and southwest; and after assembling its upland tributaries in the marshy

---

[1] *Parliamentary Papers: Egypt No. 2, 1901; Egypt No. 2, 1904,* pp. 91 ff., Garstin's reports.

basin of Lake Ambadi it proceeds eastward toward
Lake No and the Nile, but with a current which is already failing and which strays uncertainly among
many shallow *khors* and flood-spills. For a hundred
and fifty miles it wanders through hopeless wastes of
slough and fen, its waters choked with floating weeds
and polluted by decaying vegetation; a flat, unvary-
ing, treeless desolation, kept by hippopotami and
myriads of reed-birds.

When at last the Nile issues from the melancholy
regions of Lake No, it begins again to recover the
flow and dimensions of a great river. Dry land covered with thorny scrub approaches on each side, and
the bordering swamps are reduced to belts of a mile or
two. But the country stretches dead flat to the hori-
zon. In the dry season after the rank grasses have
been burned off it is as dreary as "the Norfolk coast
at low tide."[2] And during the summer floods the river
spills over its low banks and drowns vast levels of
grassland; cranes fish in the shallows, and innumerable waterfowl rise in clouds over the reedy backwaters.
The drenched land then becomes an immense and pesti-
lential swamp steaming under the African sun.

Early in July, 1898, when the river was at its
height, a small flotilla of boats and one diminutive
steamer navigated cautiously downstream from that
region of desolate and stagnant waters called Lake
No. It floated eastward past the junction of the Za-
raf, and then turned northeast down the more open
reaches of the White Nile. It passed the mouth of the

[2] *Parliamentary Papers: Egypt No. 2, 1904,* p. 100.

Sobat swollen by rains in the Abyssinian highlands, and some sixty miles farther found at last a satisfactory mooring ground on the left bank of the river.

The adventurers were a little force of one hundred and twenty Senegalese *tirailleurs* and seven French officers and noncommissioned officers under the command of Captain Marchand, all of whom had set out two years before from the Atlantic coast to reach, if possible, that very spot. Their landing-place was an insignificant elevation barely four feet above high-water, and at that time of year it was practically an island. But it was the only considerable bit of firm ground for many miles either up or down on that side of the river;[3] and it had, moreover, a place on the maps, and a name—Fashoda. Fifteen years before it had been an important post of the old Egyptian government, and the government buildings, long abandoned to the uses of the Negro villagers, were still standing. But "a more dreary or uninviting spot it is impossible to conceive."

When the expedition disembarked it had actually arrived at its chosen destination, and it therefore set about establishing itself. The flag of the French Republic was hoisted, a camp laid out, treaties were made with the Shilluk tribes,[4] and in time even a vegetable garden was planted—surely a pledge of permanent occupation. Then for security against the greatest peril in such enterprises, namely starvation, the little

[3] W. S. Churchill, *River War,* p. 396.

[4] *Parliamentary Papers: Egypt No. 3, 1898,* p. 6, Marchand to Kitchener, September 19, Treaty with Shilluks on September 3.

steamer, the "Faidherbe," was sent back along two hundred and fifty miles of river to the nearest depot of supplies at Meshra-er-Rek in the Bahr-el-Ghazelle country. Weeks passed in hopes and conjectures; but at last the tedium was broken by the sudden appearance of a hostile force.

On August 25, six weeks after Marchand's arrival, a steamboat[5] was sighted coming upstream from the direction of Omderman. It proved to be manned by a party of Mahdists, the redoubtable followers of the Khalifa Abdulla. They must have been a good deal astonished at the sight of white men where no white men should have been; and they opened fire on the French post without in the least knowing who or whence the strangers were. A sharp engagement ensued, and in the end the Arabs were forced to draw off, the upper works of their steamer (it was one of Gordon's old fleet, the "Tewfikieh") being badly pitted by the Senegalese rifle fire. But the fight had so reduced Marchand's supply of ammunition that he considered himself in a serious plight, fearing a renewal of the attack in force.[6] Fortunately, however, the Mahdists did not return. They had, in fact, gone away northward to report to their master.

Meanwhile a totally different sort of expedition was preparing against the gallant Frenchmen, and

[5] Marchand reported two steamers (*Parliamentary Papers: Egypt No. 3, 1898,* p. 6, Marchand to Kitchener, September 19, 1898).

[6] C. Mourey, "De l'Atlantique au Nil," *Annales des sciences politiques,* Vol. XIV (January, 1899).

one with which they and their one hundred and twenty riflemen could not possibly cope. On September 2 General Kitchener broke the power of Mahdism at the battle of Omderman and so opened the Sudan. The battle-field was a good five hundred miles north of the little post at Fashoda, but with a full river it was possible to cover the distance in ten days steaming or less.[7] Marchand's position had seemed incredibly remote after his adventurous journey of two years from the Atlantic coast. But as a matter of fact he was soon to find himself separated from the outer world by not more than two or three weeks of easy traveling in a new direction, that is to say northward to the Mediterranean.

Five days after the battle of Omderman the Anglo-Egyptian gunboats moored near the junction of the Blue and White Niles snapped up a prize: the little Mahdist steamer "Tewfikieh," the same which had attacked Marchand at Fashoda thirteen days before. The Arab crew had, in fact, walked into a trap. It was not until they came within sight of the shattered dome of their Mahdi's tomb that they perceived that there had been a revolution in affairs at Omderman; and it was then too late for retreat.[8]

The prisoners when questioned stated that the "Tewfikieh" in company with another steamer, the "Safieh," had gone up the White Nile a month before under orders to collect provisions; that they had es-

[7] Six hundred sixty-nine kilometers (Lieutenant-Colonel Count Gleichen, *Anglo-Egyptian Sudan*, I, 67).

[8] W. S. Churchill, *op. cit.*, pp. 389 ff.

tablished a camp and depot at Renk; and that later the "Tewfikieh," proceeding alone, had arrived opposite the old station of Fashoda, had been fired upon by black soldiers under white officers, and had been forced to turn back. The *emir* in command of the expedition had thereupon dispatched the discomfited "Tewfikieh" downriver to report at Omderman. When asked what sort of white men they had seen at Fashoda, they could not tell, being no doubt ignorant of tribal distinctions among white men; and of the flag they had observed only that it displayed bright colors. British officers who took pains to dig with their knives into the "Tewfikieh's" woodwork recovered some nickel-covered bullets, obviously discharged by modern European rifles, but giving no clue to the nationality of the mysterious invaders.[9] But however perplexed the army may have been, it is probable that the Sirdar himself was not without some inkling of the truth; for his official instructions transmitted by Lord Cromer had contained hints of possible encounters with French or Abyssinian forces farther south.[10] The German Emperor's terse comment upon the news was, "Nun wird die lage interessant werden!"[11]

On the next day, September 8, Kitchener started up the White Nile with five steamers carrying a mixed force of British and Sudanese. At Renk he scattered

[9] *Documents Diplomatiques: Haut Nil,* No. 5, French consul at Cairo to Delcassé, September 10.

[10] *Parliamentary Papers: Egypt No. 2, 1898,* p. 3, Salisbury to Cromer, August 2.

[11] *G.P.,* XIV, No. 3884, 371, *Marginal.*

the Mahdist encampment and disabled the "Safieh."[12]
On nearing Fashoda he sent forward a letter (September 18) announcing his approach; to which Marchand replied (September 19) in courteous terms, informing Kitchener that Fashoda had been occupied on July 10 by French forces and in the name of the French Republic, and that he was under instructions of his government to occupy the Bahr-el-Ghazelle to its confluence with the Bahr-el-Gebel (i.e., with the White Nile) together with the Shilluk country on the left bank of the White Nile as far down as Fashoda.[13] It would have been a preposterously huge commission for a hundred and twenty riflemen had not Europe been already long familiar with the device of skeleton occupations of vast African territories. The Anglo-Egyptian force then steamed up to the landing and the two commanders met in person.

It was the high moment in thirty years of Anglo-French rivalry in Africa; and it is not, therefore, surprising that there was some hesitation in publishing an account of so fateful an incident as that meeting at Fashoda. There was a significant silence of nearly a week. On September 20 the French government still disclaimed knowledge of Marchand's position.[14] The first news that Kitchener had arrived at Fashoda

[12] *Parliamentary Papers: Egypt No. 2, 1898,* p. 8, Rodd to Salisbury, September 22.

[13] *Parliamentary Papers: Egypt No. 3, 1898,* p. 5, Kitchener to Marchand, September 18, and Marchand to Kitchener, September 19.

[14] *London Times,* September 20.

reached the public incidentally on the 26th;[15] and meanwhile all Europe was still anxious to learn what might have occurred there. Only on the 27th came full disclosures.

During the discussions between the two commanders at Fashoda, Kitchener protested in set terms its occupation and the raising of the French flag. To which Marchand could only answer that he had received precise orders, and that it was impossible for him to retire. It looked like a deadlock. Kitchener, however, deftly evaded an open breach by inquiring if Marchand would resist the hoisting of the Egyptian flag also; and when Marchand admitted that he was in no position to resist, the Egyptian flag (but not the British) was formally raised about five hundred yards south of the French station. Kitchener then lodged a written protest against French occupation of any part of the Nile Valley, and leaving behind a Sudanese battalion under command of Colonel Jackson he proceeded south at three o'clock on the same afternoon.[16] He also took the precaution of informing Marchand by letter that the transport of war material on the Nile was prohibited.[17]

Only once thereafter and before the French finally evacuated Fashoda (on December 11) was there the slightest danger of an open rupture between the two forces cooped up together on the island—the

[15] *Ibid.,* September 26.

[16] *Parliamentary Papers: Egypt No. 3, 1898,* pp. 2–4, Kitchener to Cromer, September 21.

[17] *Ibid.,* p. 8, Kitchener to Marchand, September 21.

French in their fort at the north end and the Anglo-Egyptians in their camp at the south. So long as Marchand himself remained at Fashoda the greatest courtesy and forbearance was maintained on both sides. But a month after the arrival of the Anglo-Egyptians, in the middle of October, Marchand determined to proceed to Cairo whence communications with his home government might be more rapid and direct. During his absence Captain Germain, who had been left in command, abandoned the moderate policy of his chief and showed a more agressive front. He sent out reconnoitering parties and occupied the opposite or right bank of the river, although Marchand himself had professed to claim under his orders only the left bank. These provocative activities drew repeated protests from Colonel Jackson, who at last resorted to threats. The threats were met by defiance and there was one tense day when the French officers labored in their shirts at strengthening the entrenchments, and the Anglo-Egyptian gunboats were kept ready under steam. But at a fortunate moment Marchand returned, expressed his polite regrets, and the crisis was passed.[18] One wonders what might have been the consequence upon European destinies of even a single shot fired at Fashoda.

[18] W. S. Churchill, *op. cit.*, pp. 387 ff.

CHAPTER II

THE FRENCH EXPEDITION TO THE NILE

In November of that year (1898) the *Soleil* enumerated what might have been the benefits to France of the Fashoda enterprise: to cut the British Cape-to-Cairo route; to furnish an outlet on the Nile for the French Ubangi territories; to establish contact with Abyssinia on its western side; and finally to re-open the Egyptian question.[1]

Such may, indeed, have been the deliberate program of the French governments which in succession were responsible for the Nile expedition. But whatever may have been their ultimate objects, their instructions to Marchand were explicit only on the immediate object of the mission. The first instructions were signed on February 24, 1896;[2] and were drawn up with the approval, if not at the instigation, of the foreign minister. He was ordered to proceed to the White Nile as already planned, and to establish a good French title to the territories in that region. He was to set up friendly relations with the Mahdists, and to avoid at all costs a conflict. It was added, however, that the mission might prove difficult, inasmuch

[1] "France, Russia and the Nile" (Anonymous), *Contemporary Review,* LXXIV (December, 1898), 770.

[2] C. Schefer, *D'une guerre à l'autre,* p. 202; A. Lebon, "La mission Marchand et le cabinet Méline," *Revue des deux mondes,* March 15, 1900, p. 275.

as the Arab Mahdists were the declared enemies of the Negro chiefs who had already established relations with the French farther west.

After the Méline ministry came into power new instructions were drafted and dispatched (June 23) again defining the aims and nature of the Marchand mission: it was not to be considered as a military expedition; it must have a character *exclusivement pacifique*.[3] There must be, if not an alliance, then at least good relations with the Mahdists, who, moreover, should not be allowed to confound the French with their English rivals and should be assured of French friendliness. Here at least is an avowal of intent to establish French power on the Nile and to cultivate good relations with the African enemies of Great Britain.

But France had fostered designs on the upper Nile even earlier than the year 1896, and had disclosed her motives more plainly. As far back as 1890, De Brazza, governor of the French Congo, had appointed Liotard to occupy the Ubangi country, and to make of it a French region having an open port on the Nile.[4] In 1892 a sum of 300,000 francs had been voted for the Upper Ubangi, although the credits had never been used.[5] In 1893 President Carnot said in an interview with Monteil, an officer in French Africa, that he wished to reopen the Egyptian question, and

[3] Gabriel Hanotaux, *Fachoda*, p. 108.

[4] E. Rouard de Card, *Les territoires africains*, p. 122 (quotes *Bull. du comité de l'Afr. Fr. 1898*, p. 369).

[5] G. Hanotaux, *op. cit.*, p. 72.

that for the realization of that project it was necessary to send a French expedition to occupy some
point in Egyptian territory.[6] In 1894 the French,
watchful of their interests on the Nile, sharply protested against the Anglo-Congolese treaty of May 12
whereby Great Britain had granted the Congo certain
territories in lease along the upper White Nile, territories which, France pointed out, were still a part of
the Ottoman Empire (i.e., of Egypt), and which therefore Great Britain could not presume to barter.[7] The
Congo Agreement with France of July 14[8] was designed to replace the earlier one with Great Britain;
and France thereby scored heavily against her rival.
In the same year (1894) fresh credits were voted for
Ubangi (Fr. 1,800,000), and Monteil was sent with
orders to open a way to the Nile. He was recalled,
however, and dispatched instead against the rebel
Samory, the 1,800,000 francs being diverted to Loango and the Ivory Coast.[9]

Thus far no material progress had been made in
the White Nile schemes. It seemed for a time that the
French were becoming preoccupied elsewhere, notably
with the Niger and Lake Chad; "If there exists in fact
a question on which French public opinion is indifferent it is most certainly that of the succession to

[6] E. Velay, *Les rivalités franco-anglaises en Egypte,* p. 163.

[7] *Parliamentary Papers: Egypt No. 2, 1898,* Appendix,
p. 14.

[8] *British and Foreign State Papers,* XC (1897–98), 1279,
Franco-Congolese Arrangement.

[9] G. Hanotaux, *op. cit.,* p. 78.

Egypt in the Equatorial Province."[10] In 1895, how-ever, the authorities began at last to show a more consistent energy. In July Liotard occupied Zemio, an advance of nearly two hundred and fifty miles eastward from the confluence of the Bomu and the Welle, but still on the western side of the low Nile-Congo watershed. He passed the crest in the following year and reached Tembura well within the old Egyptian province of Bahr-el-Ghazelle. And in 1897, just before Marchand's arrival from the west coast, Liotard was in possession of Deim Zubeir, the old Egyptian headquarters and residence of Lupton Bey.[11]

It is plain, therefore, that long before Marchand embarked at Marseilles in June of 1896 the French had entertained a project of occupying the Bahr-el-Ghazelle, and that the Marchand expedition was not an isolated adventure, but was the last push in a drive eastward to the Nile.

Marchand arrived at Loango on the west coast in July of 1896. Between Loango and Brazzaville the tribes had broken out into rebellion; consequently there was a discouraging delay of six months during which Marchand fell ill and nearly died. It was not until March of 1897 that he reached the upper Ubangi—eight months consumed in pushing up the Congo and its affluents to a point from which he could really begin an advance down the east side of the central di-

[10] Henri Deherain, "La succession de l'Egypte," *Revue des deux mondes,* May 15, 1894, p. 312.

[11] Count Gleichen, *The Anglo-Egyptian Sudan,* I, 271.

vide.[12] Owing, moreover, to defective transport arrangements, his cases, which should have preceded him, did not arrive until some time later, and he suffered somewhat from shortness of supplies.[13]

He first established himself at Tembura where he built Fort Hossinger. He then selected Kojali, fifty miles northeast of Tembura, for his point of embarkation on the Sueh, which was the principal tributary of the Bahr-el-Ghazelle. There he constructed slips for repairing boats, and thence he built a road sixteen feet wide and ninety miles long back westward to the upper M'Boku. From Kojali he proceeded down the Sueh to Wau, where he built Fort Desaix. By November the expedition was established on a solid base. Two gunboats and ten barges of steel and aluminum had been launched on the waters of the Sueh in readiness for the final advance down the Bahr-el-Ghazelle.[14] It is even credible that, as was asserted,[15] had it not been for a premature fall in the levels of the Bahr-el-Ghazelle which prevented the expedition from reaching the Nile in the autumn of 1897 Marchand might have anticipated Kitchener's arrival by nearly a year.

Marchand himself, however, admitted the difficulties of his position and particularly the menace of starvation while awaiting high water to float him down stream to the Nile. The ravages of locusts had

[12] J. Darcy, *France et Angleterre: Cent années de rivalité colonial*, p. 422.

[13] A. Lebon, *op. cit.*, p. 283.

[14] Gleichen, *op. cit.*, I, 271–72.

[15] A. Lebon, *op. cit.*, p. 284.

destroyed the native plantations; and for a long time before the summer floods of 1898 the expedition had depended upon what game it could kill. "Shall we," Marchand exclaims in a letter, "be forced to eat the 'ambach' of the marshes?"[16] The hardships of Marchand's journey were perhaps no greater than those of other European enterprises in the same region. But those hardships should be particularly borne in mind. For however heroic the French exploit may have been, the very fact that it required uncommon gifts of courage and resource for white men to pass from the west coast to the Nile counted heavily against the ultimate success of French designs.

Meanwhile minor French activities elsewhere in central Africa had been timed to serve and reinforce the main effort of Marchand upon Fashoda. Marchand's instructions directed him to establish friendly relations with the Mahdists; and it is altogether likely that French agents had already found means of getting into some sort of communication with the Khalifa Abdulla at Omderman. Neufeld, while lying in chains in the Dervish capital, had heard strange tales of offers of foreign help to the Khalifa against the Anglo-Egyptian advance (1897). A field-gun had arrived from the south (perhaps through Abyssinia) as a present, together with a supply of brass cartridges.[17] In the autumn of 1898, when the Fashoda question was in controversy, the *Eclair* asserted that French action in those regions had been at the express

[16] Count Gleichen, *op. cit.,* I, 272.

[17] Charles Neufeld, *A Prisoner of the Khalifa,* p. 245.

desire of the Mahdi; and the *Journal* told of a certain
Mores who had set out for east Africa to preach a
crusade against England, and with offers of a guar-
anty of the Mahdist empire on condition of the cession of the Bahr-el-Ghazelle province to France.[18]
However that may be, the hostile reception given
Marchand by the Mahdists at Fashoda seems to show
that on that side France had achieved no solid successes.

In Abyssinia, on the other hand, the French did
gain some advantages.[19] The Abyssinian plateau dom-
inates the whole eastern side of the great valley of the
two Niles. In the region of the Sobat lofty bastions
project into the river plain to within two hundred and
fifty miles of Fashoda. It would have been not impossible, therefore, providing only they had the good will
of Abyssinia, for the French to extend a hand to Marchand from that side, thereby completely blocking the
Anglo-Egyptian advance southward. This contingency was even foreseen by the British government.

In 1896 instructions had been sent from Paris to
Lagarde, the French agent at Djibouti on the Red
Sea. He was advised that a sum of money had been
placed at his disposal and that he was expected to
spread a pacific influence in Abyssinia, and also to
press for permission to explore the Sobat through
Abyssinia and westward. In this last design he was
successful (1897). The Emperor Menelik, in his in-

[18] "France, Russia and the Nile," *op. cit.,* LXXIV, 267 ff.

[19] J. Darcy, *op. cit.,* pp. 425 ff.; Lebon, *op. cit.,* pp. 285 ff.;
Gleichen, *op. cit.,* I, 270.

terviews with Lagarde, expressed his determination to claim as his western boundary the whole course of the Nile between the fifth and the fourteenth degrees North Latitude.[20] But he feared England and was glad to accept the countenance of France; and he consented therefore to the organizing of an expedition into the west. He even attempted to persuade the Mahdists to receive as friends any white men who might enter the Sudan from the west, presumably the Marchand expedition.

In the spring of 1897 Captain Clochette headed an expedition out of Abyssinia westward toward the Nile. It was being organized while Rennel Rodd, the British emissary, was in Addis Ababa, and was to consist of two French noncommissioned officers and two hundred Abyssinians, with 200,000 rounds of ammunition.[21] After Clochette's death De Bonchamps reached the Sobat and advanced downriver as far as Nasser. But sickness, desertion, want of boats and supplies forced him to return (December 31, 1897). This expedition had marched under definite instructions to establish on the right bank of the Nile an Abyssinian fortress provisionally held by France, and on the left bank (i.e., at a point near where Marchand afterward landed) a French fortress with constant boat communication between the two. There they were to await Marchand.

Yet another attempt was made in 1898. An Abys-

[20] René Ferry, "L'Ethiopie," *Annales des sciences politiques,* XXV, 22.

[21] J. Rennel Rodd, *Social and Diplomatic Memories,* Second Series, p. 159.

sinian expedition of three or four thousand rifles accompanied by European officers descended by the Pibor and the Sobat to the White Nile. They arrived at the mouth of the Sobat toward the end of June, but they had been so weakened by fever that they returned almost immediately. It was by an irony of fortune that only ten days later Marchand's boats passed near the very spot from which they had turned back.

It must not be supposed that Great Britain remained throughout ignorant of, or indifferent to, French activities on the upper Nile. The French government very naturally refrained from publishing its intentions. But news of them got abroad, "malgré l'extrême réserve que l'on avait gardée en France."[22] As far back as 1895 (March), Sir Edward Grey, under-secretary for Foreign Affairs, was questioned in Parliament touching the rumored French advance upon the Nile. His statement in reply not only attempted to define the British position in the valley of the upper Nile, but also carried an explicit warning to France. Sir Edward declared that

the advance of a French expedition under secret instructions right from the other side of Africa into a territory over which our claims have been known for so long would be not merely an inconsistent and unexpected act, but it must be perfectly well known to the French Government that it would be an unfriendly act, and would be so viewed by England.[23]

[22] C. Mourey, *Annales des sciences politiques,* XIV (January, 1899), 59.

[23] *Parliamentary Papers: Egypt No. 2, 1898,* Appendix, p. 17; Grey, *Twenty-five Years,* I, 18. Cf. *Parliamentary Debates,* XXXII (March 28, 1895), 350.

This declaration by the British under-secretary drew from the French government a diplomatic protest and from M. Hanotaux, minister of foreign affairs, a spirited retort in the French senate (April 5, 1895), in which he scouted the British claims to a sphere of influence over vast and undefined regions, denounced as premature those "delimitations on paper" of unoccupied territories, and declared it a proceeding *peu amical* to close the question against further discussion by uncompromising claims.[24]

Again in 1897, during negotiations over the Lake Chad country, Sir Edward Monson told M. Hanotaux that Her Majesty's government would "make no difficulty" over French claims to the northern and eastern shores of the lake. But that since possession of that territory might in the future open up a road to the Nile, the British government "must not be understood to admit that any other European power than Great Britain has any claim to occupy any part of the valley of the Nile." And once again M. Hanotaux replied by making the reservations "qu'il n'a jamais manqué d'exprimer."[25] The negotiations were carried over into 1898, and eventually the British government brought themselves to propose to recognize French claims east of Lake Chad if the French would recognize English claims in the Nile Valley. But the French

[24] *Parliamentary Papers: Egypt No. 2, 1898,* Appendix, p. 20.

[25] *Documents Diplomatiques: Haut Nil,* No. 2, Hanotaux to Monson, December 24, 1897; *Parliamentary Papers: Egypt No. 2, 1898,* p. 1, Monson to Hanotaux, December 10, 1897, Hanotaux to Monson, December 24, p. 2.

could not be induced to make the exchange. Balfour complained that "they meet us by rejecting, with no excess of courtesy, the half of the proposal which is to our advantage; and then repeat without modification the other half, as if the Valley of the Nile had never been so much as mentioned between us."[26]

There the matter rested so far as diplomacy was concerned with claims on the one side and reservations on the other. It cannot be denied, however, that Great Britain had employed a tone not quite friendly and a little chauvinistic. The designs of the French government against alleged British rights were still only hypothetical. And to make a public threat of consequences to follow on a merely hypothetical offense had the look of trying to pick a quarrel. There was, moreover, a curtness scarcely to be used against a friendly power in that bald declaration of British rights as made by Sir Edward Grey; and it was likely to be as much resented by the French government as relished by the jingoes in Parliament. Baron de Courcel, the French ambassador in London, complained to the Earl of Kimberley that it amounted to a *prise en possession* of the whole basin of the upper Nile. Long afterward Grey wrote: "Looking back, I ask myself whether it [his declaration] may not have provoked the Marchand expedition."[27]

On the other hand, it must be owned that the attitude of the French government was lacking somewhat in frankness. If it had been M. Hanotaux' intention

[26] *British Documents*, I, No. 175, p. 149, Balfour to Monson.
[27] Viscount Grey, *op. cit.*, I, 20.

to deal openly with Great Britain he should have gone farther than the making of reservations. In the Final Act of the Conference at Berlin (February 26, 1885), a useful and salutary rule was laid down that powers occupying new territory in Africa should give notice to the other signatories. Great Britain had spoken plainly and perhaps too bluntly concerning her claims to the Nile Valley. France waited on events. In the Senate, M. Hanotaux expressed a hope that, when and if the time should come to fix the destinies of those remote regions, two great nations would know how to find the right formulas for conciliating their interests and safeguarding their common aspirations toward civilization and progress.[28] It was an altogether proper sentiment; but for the time it must have exactly suited his designs to keep the issue open. He seemed to deprecate "premature" settlements "on paper" as if he hoped to hurry on a French penetration of the Nile Valley, and so forestall Great Britain with a *fait accompli*.

And meanwhile the activities of French agents in Africa created an unpleasant impression in England as of something secret, oblique, and surreptitious. When in April of 1895 Kimberley had asked De Courcel for assurances from the French government that rumors were unfounded of a French expedition (it must have been that of Monteil) entering the upper Nile country, the ambassador had replied evasively that all news from those parts was tardy, and that his government could not, therefore, give assurances while

[28] C. Schefer, *op. cit.,* p. 190.

in ignorance of the facts.[29] Even when the impending crisis had been brought very close by Kitchener's victory at Omderman, M. Delcassé, who had become French foreign minister in June, 1898, intimated no more than that Marchand might be encountered somewhere on the upper Nile, and bespoke for him an attitude of restraint and consideration from the commander of the Egyptian expedition.[30] Ten days later, as the Anglo-Egyptian gunboats were approaching Fashoda, Delcassé still persisted in denying any certain knowledge of Marchand's position, although, as he was aware, the British newspapers were already asserting that the French were at Fashoda.[31]

[29] *Parliamentary Papers: Egypt No. 2, 1898,* p. 18, Kimberley to Dufferin, April, 1895.

[30] *British Documents on the Origins of the War,* No. 188, p. 163, Monson to Salisbury, September 8, 1898.

[31] *Parliamentary Papers: Egypt No. 2, 1898,* p. 4, Monson to Salisbury, September 7, 1898, and September 18, 1898, p. 6.

CHAPTER III
THE ANGLO-EGYPTIAN EXPEDITION
INTO THE SUDAN

Long before Kitchener's conquest of the Sudan Gladstone had prophesied (1877) that "England's first site in Egypt, be it by larceny or be it by emption, will be the almost certain egg of a North African Empire."[1] Only eighteen years later, and only thirteen years after the occupation of Egypt, that prophecy was about to be fulfilled. Toward the end of 1895 Lord Salisbury told the French ambassador confidentially that England proposed in concert with Egypt to prepare an expedition to subjugate the Nubian territories of the Sudan as far south as Dongola.[2]

England had traveled a long way on the road of imperialism since the beginning of Gladstone's second ministry (1880). It was only reluctantly that the Liberal government of that day intervened in Egypt,[3] and there is abundant evidence to show that neither they nor the country intended to be drawn farther into a "forward policy." The "national temper was still as hostile to expansion as when it cast out Lord Beaconsfield," and there was very little fuss made over the returned victors of Tel-el-Kebir when they paraded

[1] John Morley, *Life of William Ewart Gladstone,* III, 73.

[2] J. Darcy, *France et Angleterre,* p. 400.

[3] *British and Foreign State Papers* (1883–84), LXXV, 676, Granville to Her Majesty's representatives in Paris, Berlin, Vienna, and St. Petersburg, January 3, 1883.

the streets of London.[4] Certainly as regards Egypt's possessions in the Sudan it was hoped that all responsibility might be avoided. Gladstone declared that the Sudan had been a calamity to Egypt—a barren conquest. Lord Granville, the Foreign Secretary, laid it down that "Her Majesty's Government are in no way responsible for the operations in the Sudan which have been undertaken under the authority of the Egyptian Government" (May 7, 1883).[5] Even General Gordon, for all his talk of "smashing the Mahdi," wrote in his *Journal*, "I do not advocate the keeping of the Sudan by us, it is a useless possession and we could not govern it, neither could Egypt."[6] It was, indeed, so well understood that the Liberal government was reluctant to engage itself in the Sudan that Gordon unfairly charged them with perfidy in hoping for his speedy fall at Khartoum in order that they might be spared the necessity of sending a relief expedition.[7]

But sentiment in England had changed since those days. Tory and Liberal alike had become imperialists. When Gladstone formed his third government in 1892 he was content to leave unaltered the Tory foreign policies of 1886–92.[8] It was the Liberal under-secretary Grey who, as we have already observed, uttered

[4] J. Morley, *Gladstone,* III, 120.

[5] *B.&.F.S. Papers* (1883–84), LXXV, 682, Granville to Cartwright, May 7, 1883.

[6] C. G. Gordon, *Journals at Khartoum,* p. 168.

[7] *Ibid.,* p. 214.

[8] Viscount Grey, *Twenty-five Years,* I, 4.

the sharp warning to France in 1895 against her "un-friendly" activities in the Upper Ubangi. And the irony of the situation is that the reaction toward imperialism among Liberals was in a great measure due to Gladstone's sincere efforts to refrain from imperialism. The disaster at Majuba Hill, the Russian triumph at Penjdeh in Afghanistan, and especially the fall of Khartoum in 1885 had damaged past remedy the Gladstonian prestige, and with it the Liberalism of the Midlothian campaign had passed definitely out of favor.

The death of Gordon at Khartoum had kindled the imagination of Englishmen as few events had done in that decade; and had engendered a spirit, partly generous pride and partly vengefulness, which looked confidently toward the day of a full satisfaction to be exacted at Khartoum for the death of a hero. The motives of Englishmen for the reconquest of the Sudan were, no doubt, various.

The diplomatist said, it is to forestall the French. The politicians said, it is to score over the radicals. The ridiculous person said, it is to restore the Khedive's rule in the Sudan. But the man in the street,—and there are many men in many streets,—said, it is to avenge General Gordon.[9]

There was, indeed, much truth in Labouchere's biting paradox that the Nile had become more English than the Thames.[10]

[9] W. S. Churchill, "The Fashoda Incident," *North American Review,* CLXVII, 736.

[10] J. Darcy, *op. cit.,* p. 444.

On the side of Egypt there were also strong motives for some day undertaking a new conquest of the
Sudan. The peasantry were, no doubt, indifferent to
the recovery of Egypt's "Siberia." But its loss in
1885 had touched the dignity of the khedivial house
and called for redress. Moreover, the restless hordes
who menaced Egypt from the south rendered her frontier unsettled and its defense expensive. And, finally,
it was of paramount importance to Egypt that no un-
friendly power should be in control of the waters of the
upper Nile. It was felt that there were "scarcely two
opinions on the point that it would be an unmixed
blessing"[11] to Egypt when the matter of reconquest
was finally disposed of.

Back in 1885, however, it had seemed to responsible administrators that a generation must pass before
it would become feasible to enter upon reconquest.[12] It
is true that Egypt's financial recuperation—a prime
condition of any scheme of reconquest—had been un-
expectedly rapid. But there was as yet no apparent
necessity for haste, when in March, 1896, it was
abruptly decided in London to reoccupy Dongola.

In Egypt the British representatives were taken
utterly by surprise. There was barely time to break
the news to the Khedive before the British government's decision was communicated to the press. There
had been no adequate discussion of means, although
some inconsequential proposals had been made from
London during January and February. Rennel Rodd

[11] *Parliamentary Debates,* LX, 246.

[12] Earl of Cromer, *Modern Egypt,* II, 81.

did not believe that those who took the decision had
any intuition of how eventually fortunate it would be.
The story got about that Chamberlain had simply
asked impulsively, "Why not retake Dongola?" and
hence the instructions to Cairo. Rodd has also complained that the reconquest was initiated four or five
years before they were ready for it in Egypt; that
public works of the greatest importance had to be
postponed in favor of military expenditures.[13]

It seems evident, therefore, that the immediate
and pressing reason for undertaking the conquest of
the Sudan was not to take a theatrical revenge for
Gordon's death, nor to secure Egypt's frontier, nor
yet (as Cromer suggests)[14] to create a diversion in
behalf of the hard-pressed Italian forces in Abyssinia.
Cromer himself had made representations to the home
government that a movement from Suakin would accomplish diversion better than an expedition into Dongola. The decision sprang rather from a wish to antici-
pate the ambitions of French annexationists.[15] There,
more probably, was the real intent that lay back of
the campaigns of 1896–98; and the French were not
unaware of it. We have seen that it was not until
1895 that the French began to exert themselves with
consistent energy in an endeavor to reach the Nile. It
was in that same year (not perhaps a coincidence)

[13] J. Rennel Rodd, *Social and Diplomatic Memories,* Second
Series, pp. 85–87.

[14] Cromer, *op. cit.,* II, 83.

[15] *Parliamentary Debates,* LX, 275; Traill, *England, Egypt
and the Sudan,* p. 197; A. S. White, *Expansion of Egypt,* p. 382.

that Lord Salisbury intimated to the French ambassador the intention of his government to undertake the conquest of Dongola.

In his communication Lord Salisbury had also added that if the Anglo-Egyptian operations should later extend beyond Dongola it should be only after an understanding with the French.[16] No informed person, of course, seriously imagined that the Sudan could be conquered piecemeal. Once the march up-country was begun, no sure halting-place could be found between Wadi-Halfa and Khartoum.[17] Did Lord Salisbury intend, therefore, to imply an admission that Great Britain would consent to treat concerning the upper Nile in return, perhaps, for French recognition of the British occupation of Egypt? If that be the true implication of the British hint, then France lost by her intransigeance a great opportunity to insist on an equal right of conquest in the Sudan. But unhappily France could not bring herself to countenance Britain in Egypt. French opposition to the Anglo-Egyptian expedition into the Sudan was so intense that Berthelot, the French foreign minister, told Dufferin that the conquest of the Sudan might have "grave consequences."[18] In diplomacy it amounted to a menace, and the logical consequence of such a communiqué is an ultimatum. Bourgeois, however,

[16] J. Darcy, *op. cit.,* pp. 400–402.

[17] Cromer, *op. cit.,* II, 93.

[18] E. Velay, *Les rivalités franco-anglaises en Egypte, 1876–1904,* p. 176.

who was prime minister, disavowed the language of his colleague, and Berthelot was forced to resign.

But, short of making war, France had at its disposal in Egypt ample means of obstruction which it did not hesitate to employ. When the Salisbury government had determined to permit an expedition into Dongola it was not then intended that the British treasury should be charged with the expense. The policy was cherished that there should be an Egyptian war at Egypt's charges. But it was not sufficiently appreciated in London that the Egyptian treasury was under control, neither of Egypt nor of Great Britain, but of an international Commission of the Debt.[19]

Now when the Egyptian government applied to the commissioners for a grant of LE. 500,000 to cover the expense of the campaign, the grant was approved by a majority of four to two, and the money paid over (March, 1896). But the French insisted, not without grounds, that the payment was illegal unless unanimously approved. The French commissioner with his Russian colleague brought action against the Egyptian government. The court ordered restitution of the sums already drawn (June, 1896); and when the case was appealed it was again decided against the Egyptian government.[20]

France had thus scored a somewhat mean triumph over her rival. But she failed, nevertheless, to halt the

[19] Cromer, *op. cit.*, II, 86 ff.

[20] J. Rennel Rodd, *op. cit.*, pp. 91–107.

expedition into the Sudan. For although the Egyptian government had been forced to refrain from making expenditures out of its own resources, it immediately found at its disposal a sum of £800,000 advanced by the British treasury at 2.75 per cent. In the end, much to the disgust, it is true, of the radicals in Parliament,[21] the British grant in aid was never repaid. Nevertheless the Conservatives made out a very good case for their own policies by showing that the Salisbury government had spent less than a million (£798,802) in regaining what their predecessors had spent nine millions in losing![22] Moreover, they had the malicious satisfaction of seeing France overreach herself. The £800,000 of the British grant in aid was about one-third of the total cost of the reconquest; and France should have considered in time that if Egypt did not bear the whole cost then Britain would acquire partial rights in the conquered territory.

As might have been anticipated, the Anglo-Egyptian forces did not stop with the occupation of Dongola in September of 1896.[23] All through 1897 they prepared for a further advance. A railway was built laboriously across the Nubian desert from Wadi-Halfa to Abu Hamed, and a concentration was effected at Berber. In the spring of 1898 reinforcements of British troops were brought up to stiffen the Egyptian

[21] *Parliamentary Debates,* LX, 242, 281.

[22] *Ibid.,* LXVII, 481; *Parliamentary Papers: Egypt No. 4, 1899,* expenditure for military operations in the Sudan since January, 1883; *London Times,* January 3, 1898.

[23] W. S. Churchill, *River War,* pp. 202 ff.

army; and in April the Emir Mahmoud was beaten at the Atbara. During the summer Kitchener pressed on up-country, ferried his army across to the west bank of the river, and on September 2 met the Mahdist hosts on the field of Kerreri outside Omderman. "The Dervishes were superb,—beyond perfection."[24] But their valor was impotent against modern weapons. Their defeat was decisive, and the Khalifa Abdulla became a fugitive in the desert wilds of Kordofan. Thus we have returned once more to that memorable day (September 19) at Fashoda when Marchand and Kitchener sat confronting each other on the deck of a river gunboat, and engaged in the first parley of what was to become an international controversy.

[24] G. W. Steevens, *With Kitchener to Khartoum,* p. 282.

CHAPTER IV
THE CONTROVERSY

Fashoda stood at the intersection of two lines of European advance through central Africa: that of the French from the west, up the Congo and the Ubangi, and then down the Sueh and the Bahr-el-Ghazelle to the Nile; and that of the British from the north, up the Nile continuously, through more than ten degrees of latitude from the Egyptian frontier. For months and even years they had been converging upon the same point; and the inevitable moment of encounter must have been long a matter of anxiety to both governments. Fortunately, as that moment impended more closely, they were both aware of the necessity for infinite caution, and both set themselves to avoid, if possible, an open clash.

On the eve of the meeting M. Delcassé had informed Sir Edward Monson (September 8) that if, as seemed likely, the French expedition under Captain Marchand were met upriver, he deemed it proper that Her Majesty's government should know beforehand that the clearest instructions had been given to that officer as to his position and attitude. He had been distinctly told that he was nothing but "an emissary of civilization," without competence in the larger questions of right. And the French minister also expressed a hope that the British government would "give such instructions as would prevent a collision by reserving all questions of principle for direct discussion at home."[1] It is not unfair to suppose that these pacific sentiments of the French government were prompted by doubts of Marchand's ability to hold his own against Kitchener if it came to fighting. Under the circumstances it was only natural that they should wish to keep him at Fashoda rather by the arts of diplomacy—that is to say, by "discussion at home."

In London they seemed perhaps a trifle less solicitous about preserving the peace. Sir Herbert Kitchener was simply instructed that "nothing should be said or done which would in any way imply a recognition on behalf of Her Majesty's Government of a title to possession on behalf of France or Abyssinia to any portion of the Nile Valley."[2] But Kitchener himself exercised on the spot the greatest care and prudence. It will be remembered that on approaching Fashoda he dispatched a letter in advance "to the Chief of the European Expedition" announcing his arrival.[3] Thereby he left nothing to the hazards of a surprise meeting. And on the next day, although he at once protested in the strongest terms "the hoisting of the

---

[1] *Parliamentary Papers: Egypt No. 2, 1898,* p. 5, Monson to Salisbury, September 8; *Die Grosse Politik der Europäischen Kabinette, 1871–1914,* XV, No. 3885, p. 372, German Consul in Cairo to Foreign Office, September 11, 1898; *Documents Diplomatiques: Haut Nil,* No. 3, September 8, No. 7.

[2] *Parliamentary Papers: Egypt No. 2, 1898,* p. 3, Salisbury to Cromer, August 2.

[3] *Parliamentary Papers: Egypt No. 3, 1898,* p. 5, Kitchener to the chief of the European Expedition, September 18.

French flag in the dominions of His Highness the Khe-dive," yet he made no humiliating exactions—in fact, no exactions of any sort—which might have led to a defiance; and he was also careful to inquire whether in the face of a decidedly superior force Captain Marchand was prepared to resist the hoisting of the Egyptian flag, too, at Fashoda. Kitchener testified that "during these somewhat delicate proceedings nothing could have exceeded the politeness and courtesy of the French officers."[4] Both sides, indeed, behaved with admirable restraint; and it is impossible to decide which was the more to be commended, Kitchener for his forbearance or Marchand for his dignified yielding.

Sir Herbert Kitchener seems to have believed that Marchand's position was hopeless, and to have supposed, therefore, that the question of the title to Fashoda could be settled out of hand within a few days. In his dispatch of September 25 he pointed out that Marchand was in want of both ammunition and supplies, and that it would take months to reprovision him from the interior owing to inadequate water transport.[5] In a later telegram he suggested that if the French government would at once give Captain Marchand instructions to quit Fashoda, a special steamer could be sent to bring down the whole party. And he added that "in view of the unpleasant position in which M. Marchand and his officers are at present

[4] *Parliamentary Papers: Egypt No. 3, 1898,* p. 4, Kitchener to Cromer, September 21.

[5] *Parliamentary Papers: Egypt No. 2, 1898,* p. 9, Rodd to Salisbury, September 25.

placed, I am quite sure that no one would be more
pleased at this arrangement for their release than
they would be themselves." It may be that the Sirdar
misjudged the patriotic resolution of Marchand and
his companions; at any rate, he was too sanguine over
so easy and prompt a solution of the difficulty. The
French government declined to recall Captain Marchand.

For two months longer the dispute was carried on
between the foreign offices in Paris and London. Over
and over again pretty much the same arguments were
advanced and refuted, and with the advantage not
particularly inclining to either side in the controversy. Even after Marchand had finally (December 11)
abandoned his precarious post at Fashoda, the journals and the parliamentary debaters continued to
worry the tatters of the empty issue.

The general French contention in its simplest
terms seems to have been a claim to prior occupancy
of unoccupied territory; but with that was coupled,
most illogically, a rejection of British claims on the
ground, as will be seen, that the Bahr-el-Ghazelle was,
and had long been, Egyptian territory.

On their part the British professed, in the first instance, to be acting in behalf of Egypt, and to de-
duce their own rights in the Sudan from their special
position in Egypt. And then suddenly after the battle
of Omderman, and by a logical *volte face*, they put
forward a new claim based on conquest. It ought not
to be difficult, therefore, to convict both sides of logical incoherence. These brief statements of the ele-

ments of the controversy require, however, a fuller examination.

The territory in dispute was not, of course, the whole of the upper Nile Valley but only that part drained by the Bahr-el-Ghazelle. Its limits were indefinite, but in general they lay in a vast triangle between the White Nile on the east, the Bahr-el-Arab on the north, and on the third side the long Nile-Congo watershed running from southeast to northwest a matter of six hundred miles. Westward beyond the forbidding swamp areas lay valuable uplands, being in large part well wooded and well watered, and containing besides rich deposits of iron and copper already rudely worked by the native tribes.[6]

This region had been held for years by the old Egyptian government. The far western tableland, called Dar Fertit, had been subjugated by Zubeir Pasha, the notorious slaver and Gordon's mortal enemy, ten years before the Mahdist uprising. In 1884, however, its last governor, Lupton Bey, an ex-sea-captain turned African adventurer, had been carried away by the Dervishes to die a captive in Omderman. When about 1886 the Dervishes themselves abandoned the Bahr-el-Ghazelle, confining themselves for the most part to occasional tax-collecting forays along the Nile, the interior relapsed to the authority of the native Negro chieftains, principally Shilluks, Dinkas, and cannibal Nyam Nyams.[7] It was so remote, indeed, from the center of Dervish power at Omder-

[6] Gleichen, *The Anglo-Egyptian Sudan*, I, 156.

[7] *Ibid.*, I, 259.

man that in 1884 Gordon, before he was completely
hemmed in at Khartoum, had conceived the idea of
escaping southward with the garrison and people of
the town. And he had even written to the king of the
Belgians offering to occupy the Bahr-el-Ghazelle in
his name.[8] Some years later (in 1892–93), the Belgians of the Congo did, as it turned out, send an expedition under La Kethulle northward along the Nile-
Congo watershed as far as Hofrat en Nahas (ca. 10
N. Lat.). But in 1894 they were forced to withdraw
their few posts before a sudden inroad of Mahdists
sent to expel them. Again, however, the Mahdists
withdrew after their initial success, and again the native tribes were left to their own devices.[9]

It seems, therefore, that the French had excellent
grounds for asserting that all foreign authority had
disappeared from the Bahr-el-Ghazelle when they entered in 1895. The Belgians kept a foothold on the
Nile only far to the south, where in 1897 Chaltin had
seized Rejaf. The Mahdists were scarcely to be met
with in the whole province, and had offered formidable
opposition only when Marchand was actually established at Fashoda. And as for Egypt, its authority
had completely vanished everywhere in the Sudan after
the fall of Khartoum more than thirteen years before.
M. Delcassé was thus enabled to put forward the more
solid part of the whole French contention in these

[8] Gordon, *Journal,* p. 60; *British and Foreign State Papers*
(1883–84), LXXV, 719, Baring to Granville, February 9, 1884,
enclosing Gordon's letter.

[9] Gleichen, *op. cit.,* I, 263.

terms: "The country bordering the White Nile, though it was formerly under the Government of Egypt, had become 'res nullius' by its abandonment on the part of the Egyptian Government."[10]

This doctrine of *res nullius* could be assailed only in one point, namely the assumption that there remained no shadow of Egyptian claim. In cases of this sort, however, it often hapens that the slenderest pretensions have within them an obstinate vitality even when opposed by the plainest facts. And both the British and Egyptian governments maintained that Egypt had withdrawn from the Sudan only temporarily and under *force majeure*.[11]

Nevertheless, it was a question whether Egypt had not in reality lost everything long ago. Even Lord Salisbury admitted that her claims had been rendered dormant by the military successes of the Mahdi.[12] And there were besides certain acts and utterances in the past which seemed to show that Egypt herself had regarded her evacuation, at least in the beginning, as a definite abandonment. In 1884 Gordon had been sent to Khartoum armed with a firman "restoring the Sudan to its chiefs."[13] In that same year (June) a treaty had been arranged with Abys-

[10] *Parliamentary Papers: Egypt No. 3, 1898,* p. 1, Salisbury to Monson, October 6, 1898.

[11] "Grey at Huddersfield, October, 1898," *Liberal Magazine,* VI, 474; *Parliamentary Papers: Egypt No. 3, 1898,* p. 12, Boutros Pasha to Cromer, October 9.

[12] *Ibid.,* p. 1, Salisbury to Monson, October 6.

[13] Gordon, *op. cit.,* p. 16; Cromer, *Modern Egypt,* I, 449.

sinia providing for the cession of the Egyptian forts
by September 1 on condition of Abyssinian help in
withdrawing the beleaguered Egyptian garrisons.[14]
Again in 1884 the Khedive had informed the Porte
that he must evacuate Massowah. Italy immediately
resolved to move in, and did so without protest (February 5, 1885); Italian and Egyptian troops even
occupied the place jointly for ten months.[15] And finally in the spring of 1885 (May 15), the Egyptian
prime minister, Nubar Pasha, wrote to Emin Pasha,
the provincial governor, who was practically cut off
in the Equatorial Province, that the rising in the Sudan had obliged the Khedive's government to abandon those regions.[16] Thus in those early years Egypt
seems to have become resigned to a total loss of empire, and to have acquiesced in the bestowal of parts
of it on Italy and Abyssinia. This looked like a deliberate abandonment, and was a heavy argument
against the validity of her revived claims.

Moreover, the *res nullius* theory was confirmed in
the view of France by the activities of other powers,
and particularly of Great Britain itself, on the upper
Nile. It was contended that Marchand was at Fashoda "by the same right as the Congolese at Rejaf and
the English themselves at Wadelai,"[17] that is to say,

[14] *B.&F.S. Papers* (1883–84), LXXV, 620, Treaty between
Great Britain, Egypt, and Abyssinia.

[15] W. L. Alden, *"Erythrea," Contemporary Review*, LXXI
(January, 1897), 118.

[16] Mourey, *Annales des sciences politiques*, 1899, p. 53.

[17] *London Times*, September 14, 1898 (quotes *Temps*).

by the right of first comers in derelict fragments of the former Egyptian empire.

The Belgians had been for years sending expeditions into the upper Nile country, and with the countenance of Britain; which latter power, it was pointed out, had even presumed to lease a part of those territories to the Congo—witness the Anglo-Congolese agreement of May 12, 1894, "one of the wildest pieces of diplomatic jugglery on record."[18] The Belgians still held Rejaf which Chaltin had seized in 1897.

It was recalled also that the Imperial British East Africa Company ("Ibea") had been chartered in 1888; and that in December, 1890, Lugard had obtained the signature of the king of Uganda, in the old Egyptian "Equatoria" to a treaty for British protection. More recently there had been an ineffectual British expedition under Macdonald (1897) from Uganda northward, and another under Cavendish (1898) not yet heard from. But it could be contended that even had they been successful they would have been anticipated nevertheless by that of Marchand.[19]

It was difficult for Frenchmen to conceal a rather spiteful bitterness over British successes in Uganda. Canting English priests would bring the Word, and pushing salesmen would drive trade; while natives clad in Manchester cottons would come to sing hymns in the church at Lado.[20] It was even suggested subse-

[18] Sir Thomas Barclay, *Thirty Years Anglo-French Reminiscences*, p. 155.

[19] H. Deherain, "La succession de l'Egypte," *Revue des deux mondes*, May 15, 1894, pp. 312 ff.

[20] *Ibid.*, p. 334.

quently that Stanley's expedition to relieve Emin Pasha had been but a cunning plot on the part of England. England wished, it was supposed, to clear the Sudan of every trace of Egyptian authority as a preliminary to her own occupation. But in Equatoria Emin Pasha sustained Egyptian authority, and it followed, therefore, that England must turn him out. The rumor was floated that Emin was in peril, and on that pretext Stanley was sent to "rescue" him, although the situation in Equatoria was then *parfaitement calme*. A few months later the British flag floated over the fort at Wadelai.[21]

These imputations of craftiness and hypocrisy may have been irrelevant to the question of British rights in Uganda, but at least they were very damaging in a general way. And it is also probable that at some points British administration in central Africa was open to reproach, and particularly as regards suppression of the slave-trade. Even Stanley had testified that Great Britain "had done less than the least of all those concerned in the extirpation of the slave-trade" as carried on through British East Africa.[22]

To resume the main argument, then, if the Nile Valley were still the domain of the Khedive, by what right was Great Britain in Uganda, Italy in Senaar, or Belgium in Lado—all incontestably portions of the old Egyptian Sudan? Delcassé insisted that France was only following the example of these powers. And

[21] E. Velay, *Les rivalités franco-anglaises en Egypt,* p. 165.

[22] H. M. Stanley, *Slavery and the Slave Trade,* p. 73.

it must be admitted that the *tu quoque* argument was not without its force.

As for the special claims put forward repeatedly in the past by Great Britain to a sphere of influence of her own on the upper Nile, they had been implicitly recognized, no doubt, in the Anglo-German treaty of 1890 and the Anglo-Congolese treaty of 1894. Not only, however, were these claims incompatible with the alleged Egyptian sovereignty, but as M. Delcassé pointed out, they had been specifically met by the "reserves" which the French government had uniformly made whenever the subject was brought up.[23] The French government, therefore, "had retained for themselves the right to occupy the banks of the Nile when they thought fit."[24]

The foregoing arguments appear to be fairly conclusive in favor of the contention that until recently the Bahr-el-Ghazelle country had been *res nullius*. The French also claimed to have been the first-comers; and therein they seemed to take excellent ground. Into this region they had been steadily penetrating ever since in 1895 Liotard pushed across the portage from the upper Ubangi to the upper Sueh at Tembura in Dar Fertit. At least a year, therefore, before Kitchener opened the Dongola campaign, and three years before he arrived on the upper Nile, the French had been in actual occupation of territory drained by

[23] *Documents Diplomatiques: Haut Nil,* No. 7, Delcassé to Geoffray, September 20.

[24] *Parliamentary Papers: Egypt No. 3, 1898,* p. 1, Salisbury to Monson, October 6, 1898.

the Bahr-el-Ghazelle. In 1897 Marchand planted his farthest eastern outpost and supply-depot at Meshra-er-Rek well within the lowlands; and in July of 1898 he was already at Fashoda and had won by three months in the race against Kitchener.

But while the French were incontestably first on the ground, it was a question whether their occupation could be regarded as effective. In a letter published in France Marchand had written: "One hundred and fifty men against forty thousand! Is it not funny to the extent of side-splitting!"[25] But it was not so much funny as absurd. And therein he had touched upon the chief weakness of the French position. His "one hundred and fifty men" were utterly inadequate not only against the Anglo-Egyptian "forty thousand" but also against the powers of disease, solitude, and barbarity of the land into which they had incautiously made their way.

In France they denied reports that Marchand was short of supplies. It was reported that he had two months' rations for Europeans and four months' rations for natives, besides 28,000 rounds of ammunition.[26] Nevertheless Kitchener's account of the plight in which he found the French expedition casts a doubt over these assertions. In his report he wrote:

[25] "France, Russia and the Nile," *Contemporary Review,* LXXIV, 769.

[26] Lebon, *Revue des deux mondes,* March, 1900, p. 284; E. Rouard de Card, *Les territoires africains et les conventions franco-anglaises,* p. 171, note.

Our general impression was one of astonishment that an attempt should have been made to carry out a project of such magnitude and danger by the dispatch of so small and ill-equipped a force, which,—as their commander remarked to me,—was neither in a position to resist a second Dervish attack nor to retire; indeed, had our destruction of the Khalifa's power at Omderman been delayed a fortnight, in all probability he and his companions would have been massacred.[27]

Moreover, Marchand's following among the native Shilluks was of dubious loyalty. After the arrival of the Anglo-Egyptian forces the chief of the Shilluk tribe with a large retinue came in to Colonel Jackson's camp to pay his respects; and he entirely denied having made any treaty with the French, and expressed "the greatest delight" at returning to the Egyptian allegiance.[28] These protestations by a cunning savage may not have been entirely truthful, but at least they show that the Shilluk Mek had made up his mind that his interests no longer lay with the French commander and his little force of riflemen.

Marchand was, in truth, practically marooned on a narrow strip of dry ground surrounded by vast marshes. It seems doubtful whether at that moment he could have returned westward had he so wished. For he had with him only three small boats, the little steam

[27] *Parliamentary Papers: Egypt No. 3, 1898,* p. 4, Kitchener to Cromer, September 21; *British Documents,* I, No. 199, p. 172, Rodd to Salisbury, September 29.

[28] *Parliamentary Papers: Egypt No. 2, 1898,* p. 9, Rodd to Salisbury, September 25; *Times,* October 5; *Documents Diplomatiques: Haut Nil,* No. 18, telegram from British Agency in Cairo, September 30, 1898.

launch having been dispatched on a long and hazardous journey to Meshra-er-Rek to fetch supplies. Moreover, the Bahr-el-Ghazelle is at all times difficult to navigate, and particularly during low water.[29] In September the floods would be already dwindling, and the channel might be at any time entirely obstructed by *sudd*—jams of floating water-weeds.[30] As for land-transport, even had Marchand's resources in porters and supplies been adequate, which they were not, he would have been compelled to travel through an enormous circuit to the north and west in order to avoid the impassable marshes of the Bahr-el-Ghazelle. Even his ordinary communications were slow and extremely uncertain. It took six months for a letter from France to reach Liotard or Marchand.[31] Until Kitchener encountered Marchand at Fashoda there had been scarcely any news of him for a year or more. A letter received by his family in June, 1898, was dated from the banks of the Sueh on December 1, 1897. It was written at that hopeful moment when he was "about to embark on the Sueh for Abyssinia."[32] So isolated was he even from his own base in west Africa that after the encounter with Kitchener the French government was

[29] *Parliamentary Papers: Egypt No. 2, 1901,* p. 26, adventures of Gessi Pasha in 1880.

[30] *Parliamentary Debates,* LXVI, 330, February, 1899, Broderick: No news from Bahr-el-Ghazelle since previous December; *British Documents,* I, No. 193, p. 167, Rodd to Salisbury, September 25.

[31] Lebon, "La mission Marchand," *Revue des deux mondes,* March, 1900, p. 282.

[32] *Times,* September 14, 1898.

driven to ask permission to communicate with him through Khartoum.

In fact as the Sirdar observed in his report of September 21,

the claims of M. Marchand to have occupied the Bahr-el-Ghazelle and Fashoda Provinces with the force at his disposal would be ludicrous did not the sufferings and privations his expedition endured during their two years' arduous journey render the futility of their efforts pathetic.[33]

Marchand himself seems to have had some misgivings on the same head. While still in the West at Wau he wrote:

And then if it were only the question of pushing quickly through with my boats, it would be little. But the problem is much more difficult. One must not pass through here only. The march through a country does not constitute a right to the country traversed. It must be an effective occupation.[34]

It was all very well for an officer and a handful of men "to consecrate the rights of the first-comer" in the solitudes of the Congo or Lake Chad. On the Nile it was a different matter. There it was necessary to meet the arguments of England on points of law with even stronger arguments—by a complete military and administrative organization. Then France could have negotiated on equal terms.[35] This reasonable view

[33] *Parliamentary Papers: Egypt No. 3, 1898,* p. 4, Kitchener to Cromer, September 21.

[34] Gleichen, *op. cit.,* I, 272 (quotes *Bull. de la Soc. Geogr. de Lyons*).

[35] Darcy, *France et Angleterre,* p. 389.

must have been that of many Frenchmen, and indeed
it was unassailable.

To recapitulate, then: At the very bottom of the
French contention lay the proposition that the Bahr-
el-Ghazelle was *res nullius;* and, as already explained,
the French government rested the proof of that proposition partly on the fact of evacuation by all previous
occupiers, and partly on the acts of other powers (and
particularly of Great Britain) in appropriating elsewhere each its own bit of Nile territory. It is not likely
that Great Britain could have satisfactorily disposed
of all these arguments, although a point may have
been gained by showing that the French occupation as
actually carried out was ineffective.

Great Britain was able, however, to advance its
side of the controversy to more positive ground by insisting first on the historic claims of Egypt in the Sudan, and then upon Egypt's present economic necessities which involved complete control of the whole Nile
Valley. These two points require elaboration.

The original conquest of the Sudan was undertaken by Mohammed Ali Pasha in 1820, and was carried out with characteristic ruthlessness.[36]   All the
Arabic-speaking regions, from the Blue Nile on the
east to Kordofan on the west, were brought almost at
once under the Egyptian yoke. It was not, however,
until a generation later (1869–77) that an attempt
was made to reduce thoroughly the vast territories of
the upper White Nile—Equatoria and the Bahr-el-

[36] D. A. Cameron, *Egypt in the Nineteenth Century,* chap. xi.

Ghazelle. But thereafter and until the Mahdist revolt
'the Khedives of Egypt held sway over the whole Nile
basin from the Mediterranean to the Great Lakes.

Unfortunately for Egypt's present credit, the evidence is unanimous and explicit upon the tale of her
misdeeds during those sixty-five years of her rule.[37] A
prime reason for the original conquest was one which
held good to the end, namely, that the Sudan supplied
slaves. For two generations that unhappy land was
turned into a hunting-ground for women and children.
Egyptian officials, from the governor-general down,
and according to their means, took ventures in the traffic in human beings. The officers and men of the Egyptian army were sometimes employed in *razzias*, and received no other pay than the profits they could make
out of the expeditions. Until the days of the Khedive
Ismail no serious attempt was made to suppress these
abominations. All legitimate trade and industry had
by that time languished almost to extinction, and the
Sudan was suffering under a heartless and methodical
oppression that almost passes belief. Along the once
populous river banks north of Khartoum "there was
not a dog to howl for a lost master."[38]

True, Ismail Pasha at last made a resolute effort
to abolish the slave-trade—although not on humani-
tarian grounds, but partly because goaded by the in-
subordination of powerful slavers, and partly as a
"compliment to the European powers."[39] His own of-

[37] Baker, *The Albert Nyanza,* pp. 9–16.

[38] Baker, *Ismailia,* I, 22.

[39] *Ibid.,* I, 8.

ficials, however, were too corrupt and too deeply compromised in the trade to be trusted with its suppression, and he was forced to rely chiefly upon two in-
trepid Englishmen, Sir Samuel Baker and the ever
lamented Chinese Gordon.

The pagan Negro provinces of the south were the
chief victims of Egyptian incompetence and cruelty.
It was in the Arab and Mohammedan north, however,
that retribution first overtook a government "almost
universally hated and abhorred."[40] In August of 1881
a man named Mohammed Ahmed, a pious mystic living
on Abba island in the White Nile, proclaimed himself the expected Mahdi, and declared it his mission
to overthrow the heretical "Turks" and convert the
whole world. Religious fervor and political hatred together kindled a revolt which in less than four years
swept every vestige of Egyptian authority out of the
Sudan, and in the blindness of its fury martyred the
devoted Gordon.

Now Egypt's barbarous misgovernment of her
upper Nile provinces is wholly indefensible. But misgovernment would not of itself cloud her legal title.
Sixty-five years of undisputed possession had con-
ferred prescriptive rights which none of the powers
would have attempted to gainsay. There can be no
reasonable doubt, however, that Egypt's military reverses were conclusive of her inability to hold the Sudan. And there remained the question how that fact
was to be interpreted. In yielding to *force majeure*

[40] Cromer, *op. cit.,* I, 353 (quotes Colonel Stewart).

had Egypt definitely lost her sovereignty in the Sudan?

That might be a difficult enough question on purely theoretical grounds. But to assist in its practical answer there is the consideration that some years before the Fashoda controversy arose both France and Great Britain had made explicit affirmations of the undiminished rights of Egypt in the Sudan. The Anglo-Congolese Agreement of 1894 (May 12) has already been mentioned.[41] By that agreement Great Britain leased to the Free State for the lifetime of King Leopold the Bahr-el-Ghazelle territories stretching from the Congo watershed eastward to the Nile and northward to the 10th degree of latitude. But on the same day the signatories of the agreement and by a separate exchange of notes mutually gave "assurance that the parties to the agreement do not ignore the claims of Turkey and Egypt in the Basin of the Upper Nile."

But in spite of these admissions of Egyptian rights ("cette formule de prétérition")[42] France protested the agreement; and for this reason among others that it constituted an attack on Egyptian and Turkish rights which were based on firmans still in force and on international acts confirming the integrity of the Ottoman empire. In a memorandum by M. Hanotaux (August 8, 1894) was this passage:

[41] Gleichen, op. cit., I, 286, text of agreement.

[42] Parliamentary Papers: Egypt No. 2, 1898, p. 13, memorandum communicated by M. Decrais, August 8, 1894.

Is it necessary to mention that for many years these provinces have been occupied and administered by Egypt, and although the agents of the Khedive, in consequence of events beyond their control, have been obliged quite recently to abandon them for the moment, that the Khedivial Government has never ceased declaring its wish to reestablish its authority there?

And M. Hanotaux went on to cite the Anglo-Italian Agreement of April 15, 1891, concerning Kassala; and he pointed out that in the very body of that instrument it was declared that Egypt's rights "only remain in suspense until the Egyptian Government shall be in a position to reoccupy the district in question."[43]

To this the Earl of Kimberley replied equably that Her Majesty's government was "perfectly ready to consider whether any more explicit form of recognition can be placed on record" whereby to safeguard the rights of the Porte.[44]

Thus, in championing Egypt's claims in 1894, France had thrust herself into a position from which four years later she would no doubt have been glad to recede. Both England and France had made a point of Egypt's rights in the Sudan, but France had shown herself the more punctilious of the two. Indeed, she pressed the matter so far that Great Britain actually retracted a part of the Anglo-Congolese Agreement and did not attempt to put into effect the articles touching the lease of the Bahr-el-Ghazelle.

[43] *Parliamentary Papers: Egypt No. 2, 1898*, p. 14, memorandum communicated by M. Decrais, August 8, 1894.

[44] *Ibid.*, p. 16, Kimberley to Dufferin, August 14, 1894.

Great Britain could hardly have anticipated how convenient would prove the contentions with which France had thus troubled her. Nevertheless, Lord Salisbury did not fail to remind M. Delcassé in 1898 of the incautious arguments used by M. Hanotaux on that earlier occasion, and to point out their bearing on the theory that the Bahr-el-Ghazelle was *res nullius*.[45] By that time, however, the French government held other views. De Courcel said to Salisbury that he could not admit the strange doctrine of Egypt's perpetual estate in the Sudan, which was like the doctrine of royal legitimacy invoked by the Stuarts or the Bourbons. And he asked whether Salisbury did not consider that it was going rather far to claim for Egypt alone such imperishable rights as no other state, even in Europe, had ever asserted.[46]

But Egypt's case did not rest solely on a historic title. There was also her perennial and urgent interest in the waters of the Nile. It is a commonplace observation that Egypt's very life depends upon her river. It is therefore indisputable that whatever power controls the upper Nile is also somewhat master of Egypt's prosperity.

During the debates over Fashoda a speaker in Parliament quoted from an old letter by Sir Samuel Baker to the *Times* (October 12, 1888): "An enemy in possession of the Blue Nile and the Atbara River

[45] *Parliamentary Papers: Egypt No. 3, 1898*, p. 1, Salisbury to Monson, October 6.

[46] *Documents Diplomatiques: Haut Nil*, No. 27, De Courcel to Delcassé October 10.

could by throwing a dam across the empty bed during
the dry season, effectually deflect the stream when
risen by the Abyssinian rains, and thus prevent the
necessary flow towards Egypt."[47] It was further
pointed out that if any such danger impended in Baker's day, there was far greater cause for alarm when
the French were actually establishing themselves on
the Nile. So long as the Mahdists were strong enough
to keep out all other powers, and ignorant enough not
to attempt tampering with the Nile floods, there was
no pressing necessity to turn them out. But it was a
quite different matter when the Sudan stood as a prize
for encroaching European powers.[48]

These apprehensions may not have been altogether fanciful; for in 1893 when the French government
was planning to open a road from the Ubangi to the
Nile, a French engineer actually submitted a project
for controlling the Nile by barrages in the Bahr-el-
Ghazelle region.[49] It should be borne in mind, however,
that even had Captain Marchand been able to maintain himself at Fashoda, the French would have possessed absolute control only over the Bahr-el-Ghazelle. All other important tributaries of both the White
and the Blue Niles, as well as the main channels of
those two rivers, would have remained in the hands of
the Anglo-Egyptians. Sir William Garstin's *Reports*
of 1901 and 1904 show that the flood discharges which
are so vitally important to Egypt are drawn princi-

[47] *Parliamentary Debates,* LX, 275, Pierpont.

[48] *Ibid.,* LXVII, 476, 478.

[49] Rouard de Card, *op. cit.,* p. 122.

pally from the Atbara, the Blue Nile, and the Sobat, and not from the White Nile or the Bahr-el-Ghazelle; that even when the White Nile is free from *sudd* "some fifty per cent of its summer volume is lost in the Marshes between Bor and Lake No"; and that "the Bahr-el-Ghazelle, beyond acting as a reservoir and thus assisting the constancy of the supply, plays a very small part in the summer discharge of the White Nile, and even its flood discharge is comparatively insignificant."[50]

Any engineering works, therefore, which the French might have undertaken on the Bahr-el-Ghazelle would have affected Egypt only negatively by preventing the tapping of waters which lay stored in vast marshes westward of Lake No but which were by no means indispensable or even important to Egyptian irrigation. It is difficult to suppose that for so small an advantage the French would have dammed and diverted the Bahr-el-Ghazelle, and particularly if at enormous expense and in a region of abundant summer rains.

But while Great Britain may have been unduly disquieted over the supposed danger to Egypt's water-supply, nevertheless Egypt's permanent interest in her river required emphatic affirmation. Possession of the Sudan was what might be called an organic necessity; and it afforded a strong argument from expediency, at least, if not from law, in support of Egypt's claims.

[50] *Parliamentary Papers: Egypt No. 2, 1901*, p. 1, and *Egypt No. 2, 1904*, pp. 143–44.

These claims of Egypt in the Sudan, based partly on ancient rights and partly on present necessities, were now made to face two ways. It was held that they excluded French rights on the one hand and implied British rights on the other. At least it was in that sense that the British government invoked them in its own behalf. But even granting that Great Britain had made a good case for Egypt, did it follow therefrom that any color of right had been thrown over her own pretensions?

It is true that Great Britain had put itself in a position of peculiar responsibility as between Egypt and the Sudan. It will be remembered that just before the beginnings of the Mahdist revolt England had occupied Egypt. In both Egypt and the Sudan the British government had wavered irresolutely between two incompatible policies: that of restoring order and that of evacuation. In the Sudan as in Egypt the political skies passed through so many rapid changes that, to use Lord Granville's own figure against himself, the British government seemed to be constantly employed in putting up its umbrella and taking it down again.[51] They ended by staying in Egypt and abandoning the Sudan, but not before they had more than once changed their minds.

Early in the Mahdist rising the Egyptian government had cherished hopes of weathering the storm which still hung as a distant portent over the deserts of Kordofan. The British government was skeptical but, willing at first to evade responsibility, it had in-

[51] Granville in Lords, Hansard, CCLXXXIV, 30.

formed the Egyptian minister, Cherif Pasha, through Sir Edward Malet (May 7, 1883) that "Her Majesty's Government are in no way responsible for the operations in the Sudan. . . . ."[52] It was a futile handwashing. And very soon it was seen that Egypt must be told plainly to give up her empire. Abandonment was "very unpalatable to the Egyptian Government."[53] Nevertheless, Granville wrote to Baring, the British representative at Cairo (January 4, 1894), "that it will be necessary that those ministers and governors who do not follow this course will cease to hold office."[54] After that there could be no more quibbles and evasions regarding British responsibility for the evacuation of the Sudan in 1885.

It is equally certain that the reconquest of 1896–98 was initiated and carried through on the moral if not the legal responsibility of Great Britain. Egypt would never have ventured alone upon so momentous a step.[55] The military operations were nominally conducted under the Egyptian flag, and the commander-in-chief, though an Englishman, was Sirdar of the Egyptian army. But the very decision to reconquer was taken in London, and not in Cairo, and rested, in part at least, on considerations foreign to the interests of Egypt.

[52] *B.&.F.S. Papers* (1883–84), LXXV, 682, Granville to Cartwright, May 7, 1883.

[53] Cromer, *op. cit.,* I, 378.

[54] *B.&F.S. Papers* (1883–84), LXXV, 703, Granville to Baring, January 4, 1884.

[55] Cromer, *op. cit.,* II, 113.

But did responsibilities entail privileges? The French had all along maintained that the authority of England in Egypt rested on a basis of fact, not of right. It could have been argued, therefore, that no British rights in the Sudan were deducible from a British occupation of Egypt.[56] It was contended, moreover, that even a specific mandate from Egypt was not valid unless confirmed by the sultan of Turkey as suzerain.[57] This last contention, that the Porte should have been consulted, was perhaps too fine-drawn and lawyerlike. For by the Turkish firman of 1873 (renewed in 1879) the independence of the khedives had been made practically absolute, subject only to the annual tribute. Nevertheless, it must be admitted that the rights claimed by Great Britain for herself in the Sudan were open to question so long as they rested in the main merely upon an alleged transfer of rights from Egypt.

Suddenly, however, Great Britain was enabled to mend her position. Kitchener's victory at Omderman on September 2, 1898, furnished newer, more direct, and more candid justification for England's presence and pretensions in the Sudan than did the rights of Egypt claimed vicariously. Thereafter and to the very end of the controversy, Great Britain frankly claimed the rights of a victor.

[56] *Documents Diplomatiques: Haut Nil,* No. 25, De Courcel to Delcassé, October 5, 1898.

[57] Rouard de Card, *op. cit.,* p. 166; *Documents Diplomatiques: Haut Nil,* No. 7, Delcassé to Geoffray, September 20, 1898.

Even before Kitchener found Marchand at Fashoda Lord Salisbury had written to Sir Edward Monson
(September 9) to inform M. Delcassé that "by the
military events of last week all territories which were
subject to the Khalifa passed by right of conquest to
the British and Egyptian Governments. Her Majesty's Government do not consider that this right is
open to discussion. . . . ."[58] And, again, two months
later in a Guildhall speech Lord Salisbury declared
that as the victory of Lord Wolesley at Tel-el-Kebir
had altered the British position in Egypt, so the victory of Kitchener at Omderman had altered their position in the Sudan.[59] The analogy may not have been
perfect, for Great Britain had not claimed to conquer
Egypt in 1882. But at least it was a straightforward
and refreshing declaration that so far as Britain was
concerned possession was nine points in the law and
could not be gainsaid, whether in Egypt or the Sudan.

It may be useful to quote in full Lord Salisbury's
statement to the French ambassador:[60]

I pointed out to him that the Egyptian title to the
banks of the Nile had certainly been rendered dormant by
the military successes of the Mahdi; but that the amount
of right, whatever it was, which by those events had been
alienated from Egypt, had been entirely transferred to
the conqueror. How much title remained to Egypt and how

[58] Parliamentary Papers: Egypt No. 2, 1898, Salisbury to
Monson, September 9; Documents Diplomatiques: Haut Nil, No.
4, telegram from Salisbury, September 9.

[59] Liberal Magazine, VI (1898), 518, extract from Salisbury's
speech of November 9, 1898.

[60] Parliamentary Papers: Egypt No. 3, 1898, p. 1, Salisbury
to Monson, October 6.

much was transferred to the Mahdi and the Khalifa, was, of course, a question which could be practically settled only as it was settled, on the field of battle. But their controversy did not authorize a third party to claim the disputed land as derelict. There is no ground in international law for asserting that the dispute of title between them, which had been inclined one day by military superiority in one direction, and a few years later had been inclined in the other, could give any authority or title to another power to come in and seize the disputed region as vacant or relinquished territory. To the last the power of the Dervishes was extended as far south as Bor, and their effective occupation did not cease till their title passed by the victory of Omderman without diminution into the hands of the conquering armies.

But Lord Salisbury was not permitted thus to take fresh ground unchallenged. It was very soon pointed out that this new head of debate was inconsistent with previous arguments. In the British Commons the radicals voiced their displeasure. The mask had been dropped at last, declared Morley; the vindication of Egypt's claims was no more than a pretext since now Great Britain had announced that her title was that of conquest.[61] An article in the *Liberal Magazine* argued in the same sense: Lord Salisbury had said that Great Britain held the dominions of the Khalifa by two titles, by the rights of Egypt and by the right of conquest. But to hold by the right of conquest implied that the right of the vanquished was good, and hence there could have been no Egyptian rights.[62]

---

[61] *Parliamentary Debates,* LXVII, 461, February 24, 1899.

[62] *Lib. Mag.,* VI (1899), 100.

In Paris M. Delcassé may have been taken somewhat off his guard by Lord Salisbury's *démarche*. He
read over three or four times Sir E. Monson's paper
which contained the British government's first assertion of the right of conquest. He did not immediately
attempt a full refutation, but only observed that the
expression "territories of the Khalifa" which he found
in the communication was a vague form of words, and
that "he certainly himself had no accurate knowledge
of their extent."[63]

It was, however, a shrewd reply. If it could be
shown that the Bahr-el-Ghazelle was not subject to
the khalifa, then claims drawn from the right of conquest would be at once disposed of so far as that region
was concerned. De Courcel argued to Salisbury that
the Bahr-el-Ghazelle could hardly be said to have be-
longed to the Mahdists, since for some years French
posts had been established there and since Marchand
had met no Mahdist forces until he reached the Nile.[64]
It was to defeat this line of reasoning, no doubt, that
Lord Salisbury (as already quoted) later informed
the French ambassador that "to the last the power of
the Dervishes was extended as far south as Bor," i.e.,
many hundred miles south of Fashoda.

But whatever may have been the defects of a claim
based on conquest, it must have had great merits in the
eyes of the British government. At a stroke it accom-

[63] *Parliamentary Papers: Egypt No. 2, 1898,* p. 6, Monson
to Salisbury, September 12, 1898.

[64] *Documents Diplomatiques: Haut Nil,* No. 30, De Courcel to Delcassé, October 12, 1898.

plished two things. In the first place, it cut through all the flimsy paper arguments. It was an appeal to the fact of "forty thousand men" with abundant stores and arms, a railway at their backs, and a fleet of gunboats to carry them upcountry, as against eight Frenchmen and one hundred and twenty Senegalese at Fashoda. "But for the reconquest of the Sudan there would have been no Fashoda incident at all";[65] for, it was argued, Marchand could not have held out.

In the second place (and this is rather more important), it relieved Great Britain of the inconvenient fiction that the Sudan war was a purely Egyptian enterprise. It was a fiction which in the beginning may have had its roots in fact, and which certainly had its uses in baffling French obstructionism in Egypt. But it had been a clumsy device at best, and toward the end of the war it was notoriously inconsistent with the real situation. Now, therefore, Britain stood forth in her true light as a partner in the reconquest of 1896–98; and it might be even contended that she was an equal partner, in spite of the fact that Egypt contributed by far the greater proportion in men and money. It has already been noted that the British treasury furnished only about one-third of the total expense of the war;[66] and it was not until the spring of 1898 that British troops arrived at Berber to take part in the

[65] Asquith at Keighley, October 22, 1898; *Lib. Mag.,* VI (1898), 478.

[66] *Parliamentary Papers: Egypt No. 4, 1899,* expenditure for military operations in Sudan.

campaign.[67] But it is almost incredible that the lost provinces would have been recovered even in our own day had not Great Britain furnished at the proper moment not only men and money but still more valuable assistance in diplomacy and, above all, in moral energy. While, therefore, Egypt's share in the enterprise of reconquest may be exactly expressed in terms of battalions and pounds, Great Britain's contributions may not be so precisely enumerated or estimated, but were nevertheless innumerable and inestimable.

A review of the whole British case, then, would stand somewhat like this: British claims rested in the first instance upon Egyptian rights, for which Great Britain was trustee. Those rights had never been forfeited. But even if it were admitted that Egypt's rights had lapsed, then they must have been transferred to the Mahdists—unless, indeed, it was to be supposed that they had passed to no one in particular, an implication of the *res nullius* theory. Now, however, the Mahdists had been conquered by combined British and Egyptian forces; and thus the old Egyptian rights had been vindicated and Great Britain had acquired fresh rights of her own.

This is not, indeed, a perfect piece of reasoning, but in the end it served. For the settlement of the controversy was to rest, not upon a well-drawn brief, but upon many obscure calculations, in which armaments and alliances counted for more, no doubt, than did logic.

[67] Cromer, *op. cit.,* II, 97.

CHAPTER V

THE FRENCH SURRENDER

Meanwhile public opinion on both sides of the channel was not silent. A year before there had been a momentary flush of kindness between France and Great Britain. At the Queen's Jubilee the Duc d'Auerstadt, who was present at the celebrations, was welcomed with great heartiness. And in the spring, when the Queen was on her way to the Riviera, she had a friendly interview with M. Faure.[1] But the Fashoda incident renewed once more the old tension of ill-will, and the strain upon pride and temper became dangerously severe.

In England the heat of feeling was perhaps not to be quite accounted for in its occasion. There was "a volume of opinion in Great Britain favorable to the maintenance of the Egyptian territories on the Upper Nile wholly disproportionate to the value of those regions."[2] Morley declared in a speech at Brechin (January, 1899) : "I do not believe in all the unblessed annals of Jingoism, there was ever an instance where the excitement or the uproar so outstripped the necessities of the case."[3] And Morley found association even

[1] Lawton, *Third French Republic.*

[2] W. S. Churchill, "The Fashoda Incident," *North American Review,* CLXVII, 743.

[3] *Liberal Magazine,* VII (1899), 14, extract from Morley's speech on imperialism.

with the Liberal party distasteful, drunken as they were with the foolish wine of imperialism, "that heady gospel of expansion at any cost."

This intense outburst of feeling is to be explained partly as a revulsion against the old humiliating policy of "graceful concession." For once the Government seemed to be acting strongly and consistently, and the whole country rose to support them. Salisbury had actually dared to be brave. After the full disclosures of the Fashoda papers relief was felt and expressed that British rights were not to be "frittered away by negotiations, however ably conducted."[4]

But in addition to the imperialistic exultation, there was in English minds also a sense of deep resentment against France for what was judged to be a deliberate and gratuitous affront, a malicious trick. Great Britain had without concealment undertaken to conquer the Sudan; a step dictated, it was said, by national honor and by national responsibilities in Egypt. France, for no reason beyond greed for territory, had sought to forestall that design. It seemed there could be no excuse for the treachery of that secret expedition to Fashoda. This belief that France was incorrigibly hostile and envenomed toward England made any concession appear to be merely an act of credulous folly.

The extreme measures resorted to by Lord Salisbury against France can, indeed, only be justified by the indubitable hostility and unlawfulness of the French provocation. Even the gravity of the interests at stake would not excuse his scarcely veiled abandonment of the *ter-*

[4] Duke of Devonshire, at Glasgow, October 18, 1898; *Liberal Magazine,* VII (1898), 484.

rain of diplomacy if France had acted in good faith or if her intentions could have been shown to have been free of conscious antagonism to this country.[5]

In France, too, there was a great deal of bitterness and outcry, some of it immoderate. Absurd charges were made, as, for instance, that Great Britain was at the bottom of the Dreyfus affair.[6] But the tone of the press was for the most part courteous and conciliatory, even when advancing inadmissable claims. And its attacks were not so implacable or concerted as might have been expected: "There is none of that disciplined uniformity in their utterances which marks the well-trained squadrons across the Rhine."[7] Moreover, the anti-British indignation was to be met chiefly among the intellectuals. Among the masses of France there seemed to be room for only one great enmity. "Que ça nous fait Egypte?" exclaimed a workingman. "Anglais! c'est pas prussiens."[8]

Nevertheless, the temper of the two countries, and particularly of Great Britain, was dangerous. Hicks-Beach, who spoke as a minister of the crown, declared that Great Britain would recoil before nothing, an ominous utterance. English merchants in Paris held new orders in suspense, and standing orders were not executed. Business was almost at a standstill for a few days in September. The French fleet was ordered

---

[5] "Diplomaticus," "Fashoda and Lord Salisbury's Vindication," *Fortnightly Review,* LXIV (November, 1898), 1003.

[6] "France, Russia and the Nile," *Contemporary Review,* LXXIV, 777 (quotes *Le petit journal*).

[7] *Times,* September 21 and 29.

[8] Barclay, *Thirty Years Anglo-French Reminiscences,* p. 160.

to Cherbourg during the negotiations. It steamed through the straits of Gibraltar with lights out. May-ors of the channel ports were ordered to requisition churches for hospitals, and to report on beds and am-bulances. Stores and ammunition were collected at Cherbourg. Orders to march were in the hands of all commanding officers. And in Britain, too, there was a flurry of warlike preparation. The fleet was sent to Alexandria to protect the Suez Canal, and at Ports-mouth they had one of their "fire-brigade trials."[9]

Truly, when matters had come to such a pass war was in plain prospect. Six months later Mr. Labou-chere declared in the British Commons that Great Britain had been calm over the Fashoda incident, be-ing convinced that two great civilized nations would not go to war "over a miserable swampy bog some-where in the middle of Africa."[10] But it is questionable whether in the previous autumn those comfortable convictions had been much entertained. Indeed, it looked very much as if one side or the other must per-mit itself to be overborne if an armed conflict was to be avoided. Among neutrals there seemed to be an opin-ion that French persistence would win—that the Brit-ish Government could be squeezed as on other occa-sions, and would surrender its rights in the interests of peace. It was admitted that the British position on the Nile was strong. But so had it been on the Niger before the Anglo-French agreements of June, 1898.[11]

[9] *Ibid.,* p. 145.

[10] *Parliamentary Debates,* LXVIII, 648, March 13, 1899.

[11] *Times,* September 30, *re* Austrian press.

This time, however, M. Delcassé had tested for himself the stiffness of Salisbury's resistance.

It is hardly surprising that Lord Salisbury once exclaimed in a spirit of petulance that "Africa was created to be the plague of the Foreign Office."[12] Here in that unhappy continent was a state of things mischievous enough to distract not one but two foreign offices. France and England were caught fast in a deadlock; and for a time it seemed that each side had persuaded itself that the issue was supreme and no retraction possible.

M. Hanotaux has made an interesting estimate of the character and methods of diplomacy in France and England. The English diplomat, he judges, is "solide, d'aplomb et plein de sens," extremely prudent and visibly tied to instructions. The French diplomat, on the other hand, is more capricious because he hunts for general arguments. "Le négociateur français veut convaincre, tandis que le négociateur anglais se contente de vaincre."[13] That is to say, for the Frenchman diplomacy is the art of perfecting an argument while for the Englishman it is a practical matter of winning the case. Whether or not this be true as generalization, it does seem to point the difference between French and British diplomacy in the final settlement of the Fashoda question. While the French held language rather of remonstrance and deprecation, raised general questions, seemed to count upon the privilege of leisurely negotiation, spoke more than once of pa-

[12] *Liberal Magazine,* November, 1897, p. 480.

[13] Hanotaux, *Fachoda,* p. 85.

tience and conciliation, the British Foreign Office held a high tone, forced the pace, declined to discuss. They were not so much like lawyers resting their case upon evidence as like impatient litigants who were prepared to terminate the dispute by pocketing the title-deeds, come what might. They seemed, in short, resolute *de vaincre.*

The British government was more than steadfast; it was almost peremptory. There are, for instance, these passages from the correspondence between Salisbury and Monson: "Her Majesty's Government do not consider the right of conquest open to discussion."[14] And again some days later (September 18) : "It was right that I should state to him categorically that they [the British Government] would not consent to a compromise,—'on ne consentira jamais à transiger,'—on this point."[15] In London Lord Salisbury intimated to the French ambassador (October 30) that "so long as M. Marchand floated the French flag at Fashoda any discussions between the British and French Governments upon frontier questions in that region were impossible, for if we took part in them we should be admitting the legality of M. Marchand's position."[16] Delcassé seems to have felt, perhaps resentfully, that he was being driven too hard. On September 27 Monson was pressing him urgently to say

[14] *Parliamentary Papers: Egypt No. 2, 1898,* p. 5, Salisbury to Monson, September 9.

[15] *Ibid.,* p. 6, Monson to Salisbury, September 18.

[16] *British Documents,* I, No. 223, p. 187, Salisbury to Monson, October 30.

whether he refused at once to recall Marchand. "After considering his reply for some few minutes, his Excellency said that he himself was ready to discuss the question in the most conciliatory spirit, but I must not ask him for the impossible." Monson on his part only reiterated the assertion that "there could be no discussion upon such questions as the right of Egypt to Fashoda."[17]

In these last pressing moments, therefore, Great Britain refused to be drawn into a discussion of her two main contentions: the rights of Egypt and the rights of conquest. But without discussion no refutation by Delcassé was possible. Diplomacy was impotent if it was not to be permitted to have its say. It looked to Delcassé as if he were being asked to yield his case unheard. The French were the first at Fashoda, they had taken it from the barbarism, from which two months later Great Britain snatched Khartoum. To ask them to abandon it before discussion, that would be "au fond, formuler un ultimatum.—Eh bien! qui donc, connaissant la France, pourrait douter sa réponse?"[18] He told Monson that he did not propose to keep Fashoda in the teeth of everything; "but can we submit to be summoned to abandon it without discussion. . . . ?"[19] Nevertheless, he was making some gal-

[17] *Parliamentary Papers: Egypt No. 2, 1898,* p. 11, Monson to Salisbury, September 27; British Documents, I, No. 196, p. 170; Monson to Salisbury, September 28; *ibid.,* I, No. 209, p. 179, Monson to Salisbury, October 11.

[18] *Documents Diplomatiques: Haut Nil,* No. 22, Delcassé to Geoffray, October 3, 1898.

[19] *Ibid.,* No. 24, Delcassé to De Courcel, October 4, 1898.

lant efforts to placate England and break through the *impasse*.

It will be remembered that some days before the encounter between Kitchener and Marchand, M. Delcassé had hoped to prevent an armed clash at Fashoda by representing Marchand as merely an "emissary of civilization." It was hardly a well-considered artifice. For, as was pointed out, if Marchand were no more than an adventurous explorer in difficulties among the swamps of the upper Nile, it was strange that the French government should be at such pains to keep him in that cruel position. On the 18th of September, however, M. Delcassé found a new explanation of the status of Captain Marchand: Great Britain was asked to believe that the presence of Marchand in Fashoda was not meant as a deliberate provocation. He told Monson that "as a matter of fact, there is no Marchand mission." True, there had been a Liotard mission in 1892–93. Marchand was a subordinate of, and had his orders from, Liotard. If he, Liotard, had employed Marchand to extend French authority to the Nile in 1896–98, his action was only in pursuit of a design begun in 1892, that is to say, antecedent to Sir Edward Grey's warning in the Commons.[20] The implication of this statement, repeated more than once, seemed to be that there could not have been any question of an "unfriendly act" in the sense of Grey's declaration. This exposition of the relations of Marchand

[20] *Parliamentary Papers: Egypt No. 2, 1898,* p. 6, Monson to Salisbury, September 18; *Documents Diplomatiques: Haut Nil,* No. 7, Delcassé to Geoffray, September 20, 1898.

to his government seems, however, to have been little more than an attempt to trail a herring across the path of the negotiations. The quibble it contained was too transparent to be of much use in turning the edge of British indignation. It was given up. Marchand was officially recognized by promotion to the rank of major,[21] which was at once a recompense to a brave soldier and an avowal of complicity in his exploits.

In his extremity M. Delcassé appears to have attempted to temporize. The French government had not yet heard officially from Captain Marchand. Permission was therefore asked to communicate directly through Cairo.[22] There seems to be little doubt that a hope was entertained of prolonging the negotiations on the basis of Marchand's version of the situation at Fashoda. If that was the motive it was frustrated. The request for permission to communicate through Cairo was, indeed, granted, but with stipulations which robbed it of all advantage to the French government. Monson was directed to state to M. Delcassé "that the fact of Her Majesty's Government having complied with his Excellency's request in regard to the transmission of the message does not imply the slightest modification of the views previously expressed by them."[23] Moreover, it was a move which turned out

---

[21] *Times,* October 3, 1898; *Documents Diplomatiques: Haut Nil,* No. 17, Delcassé to French consul in Cairo, September 30, 1898.

[22] *Ibid.,* No. 13, Delcassé to Geoffray, September 28, 1898.

[23] *Parliamentary Papers: Egypt No. 2, 1898,* p. 12, Salisbury to Monson, October 3.

badly for the French. Marchand somewhat exceeded his orders, and himself proceeded downcountry in order to communicate more easily from Cairo. Delcassé was furious that he had quitted his post; it was "incredible, unpardonable."[24] And it even occurred to the British to profit by the captain's ill-advised step by keeping him at Cairo. Salisbury concurred with the Sirdar in urging that the gunboat which was waiting at Khartoum for Marchand's return should be sent back upcountry without delay, so that the British authorities in Egypt might truthfully say that there was no boat starting south for some time.[25]

Nevertheless, M. Delcassé experimented a little with compromise. On October 12 the French ambassador offered a suggestion that France should retain an outlet on the Nile by keeping a post on the upper Bahr-el-Ghazelle.[26] It was a concession urged upon the British by some persons outside of government in both England and France. It was argued that such an arrangement ought not to be more difficult to effect than had been a similar one on the Niger (August, 1894). Leroy-Beaulieu asserted that rivers were natural frontiers, for example the Ubangi between the French and Belgian spheres in the Congo.[27] The Nile, it was said, had long been considered the "terme nor-

[24] *British Documents,* I, No. 222, p. 186, Monson to Salisbury, October 29.

[25] *Ibid.,* No. 224, p. 187, Salisbury to Cromer, October 30.

[26] *Parliamentary Papers: Egypt No. 3, 1898,* p. 9, Salisbury to Monson, October 12.

[27] *Times,* September 30.

mal de notre expansion vers l'est"; and as for the watershed between the Congo and the Nile it was so low and vague that it made no clear dividing line.[28]

These suggestions were perhaps not unreasonable; although, to be sure, it should have been remembered that the unsuccessful Bonchamps mission from Abyssinia seemed to indicate that not the Nile but some other point farther east (perhaps Djibouti on the Red Sea) had been the original *terme normal* of French expansion. However that may be, it is likely that the real objection to these proposals was that they contemplated not compromise but a surrender by Great Britain. The substance of the whole controversy was just whether France should have a door on the Nile, and it is improbable that Great Britain seriously entertained the notion of conceding even the semblance of what was asked. At any rate, Lord Salisbury looked on the matter with a cold eye. He complained of the French ambassador that

the extreme indefiniteness of his language and the rhetorical character he gave to it by the great earnestness with which he addressed himself to that subject, made it impossible for me to express or to form any definite opinion upon the various propositions which he seemed to desire to convey.[29]

In these hard circumstances M. Delcassé at last gave way. He had fought an admirable rearguard action. Perhaps he had already too long delayed his sur-

[28] Mourey, "De l'Atlantique au Nil," *Annales des sciences politiques*, 1899, p. 51.

[29] *Parliamentary Papers: Egypt No. 3, 1898,* p. 9, Salisbury to Monson, October 12.

render. That was the opinion of Münster, the German ambassador in Paris, who believed that if Delcassé had only from the first realized that he was in an untenable position and had retreated betimes he might have spared France and himself a humiliation.[30] There need not in that case have been any talk of war, and France would not have seemed to give way under duress. And, besides, the Marchand mission was not Delcassé's own measure; it was a legacy from the previous administration, and it would seem that he might have promptly denied responsibility for it and abandoned it without much straining the principle of loyalty. Now, however, he had got himself into a position from which there was no escape except by a mortifying submission. He had once used brave words to Monson: that in his hands the national honor could not be touched.[31] He may have consoled himself now with Lord Rosebery's half-humorous reflection that "after all, a flag was a very portable object," and that in this present case, the national honor was also not immovably fixed in space. At any rate, it is much to his credit that he drew back from extreme expedients. On November 4, 1898, the following announcement appeared in the French papers: "Le gouvernement a résolu de ne pas maintenir à Fashoda la mission Marchand. Cette décision a été prise par le conseil des ministres après un

[30] *Grosse Politik,* XIV, No. 3903, p. 384, Münster to Foreign Office, November 3; No. 3892, p. 376, Münster to Hohenlohe, October 17.

[31] *Documents Diplomatiques: Haut Nil,* No. 22, Delcassé to Geoffray, October 3, 1898.

examen approfondi de la question. . . . ."[32] Orders were telegraphed to the French ambassador in London to inform Salisbury that Fashoda would be evacuated; that the Marchand mission had ceased to have a political significance.[33] Accordingly, on December 11 Marchand quitted Fashoda carrying with him the flag of the dervish emir who had fought against him at Fashoda, a trophy which, however, had been presented to him as a mark of respect by the Eleventh Sudanese Regiment of the Egyptian army, who were the real victors.[34]

[32] Darcy, *France et Angleterre,* p. 441.

[33] *British Documents,* I, No. 226, p. 188, Monson to Salisbury, November 3, and I, No. 227, Salisbury to Monson, November 4.

[34] J. Rennel Rodd, *Social and Diplomatic Memories,* p. 242.

CHAPTER VI

THE SETTLEMENT

Unfortunately the recall of Marchand did not at once settle the issue. The implications of evacuation had still to be defined. It will be remembered that the French held other posts in the Bahr-el-Ghazelle country—at Meshra-er-Rek, at Wau, at Tembura, and clear back to the Ubangi headwaters. They had been in established possession of some of these places for months and even years. The French government had as yet conceded no more than the evacuation of Fashoda. Wherefore, even if the French had made up their minds, as might reasonably be supposed, to resign all Nile territories to which Britain made pretensions, it was still necessary to determine the limits of those territories.

Baron de Courcel had vainly tried (October 5) to have an understanding on these matters while yet the French occupied the vantage point of Fashoda. "To what place should Marchand withdraw?" he asked. "Where arrest his march? Where are the limits of England's pretensions, either for herself or for Egypt?" It was indispensable, he said, that the evacuation of Fashoda, if it ought to take place—which he did not absolutely refuse to admit for argument's sake —should yet be preceded by an agreement on its mode and its consequences.[1] In raising a question of the fu-

[1] *Documents Diplomatiques: Haut Nil,* No. 25, De Courcel to Delcassé, October 5, 1898.

ture, De Courcel was perhaps only attempting prudently to meet difficulties by anticipation, a very proper function of diplomacy. From his tone of vehement
expostulation, however, it seems probable that he was
expressing simply a natural disinclination to surrender at discretion. But Salisbury, as always, refused
to be drawn into a discussion of remoter issues, being
no doubt convinced, and perhaps rightly, that Fashoda alone decided all. Nevertheless the ultimate consequences of the evacuation had still to be discovered.
For more than two months there was a cessation of
diplomatic exchanges on the matter of the Bahr-el-
Ghazelle, and all the residual issues hung indetermi-
nate, not quite neglected and certainly not forgotten,
but yielding no formal discussions. A settlement had
still to be made.

Meanwhile the British cabinet seemed to be in a
temper quite as unaccommodating after as before the
evacuation of Fashoda. It was believed, indeed, that
Lord Salisbury was inclined to concede some compensation to France as a solace to her wounded pride, but
that he could not overcome the objections of his colleagues, and particularly of Chamberlain and the
Duke of Devonshire, who seemed to be convinced that
France would still try to play them some low trick.[2]

For months there had been apparent in the British
cabinet the inconveniences of this dualism between Salisbury, on the one hand, who was growing older and
more indolent than he used to be, and who felt an aver-

[2] *Grosse Politik,* XIV, No. 3925, p. 405, Hatzfeldt to Hohenlohe, December 22, 1898.

sion to adventures whether in diplomacy or war, and Chamberlain, on the other, "pushing Joe," the Colonial Secretary, inclined perhaps to go too fast in everything, whose great influence in foreign politics, while not formal was nevertheless actual.[3] The prime minister hinted to Hatzfeldt, the German ambassador, that in Chamberlain he had to do with a *Durchganger* who knew neither measure nor limit.[4] And Chamberlain, on his side, had acquainted another German confidant with his opinion that Lord Salisbury himself had not the strength of mind for an energetic policy toward France, as had Bismarck at Ems.[5]

In Parliament, of course, there had always been a hardy minority opposed to the imperialistic courses of government. Long ago reasons of humanity had been urged against the subjugation of the Sudanese: they should be left, rather (in Gordon's phrase), as God had placed them. Reconquest was an act of aggression, not of defense.[6] And now in the winter of 1899 there were still those who were not to be silenced even by the manifest success of the enterprise. John Redmond gave notice (February 20) that the Irish members in Parliament would oppose a grant of £30,000 to General Kitchener "on the ground of the outra-

[3] *Ibid.,* XIV, No. 3801, p. 244, Hatzfeldt to Hohenlohe, June 3, 1898; *British Documents,* I, No. 154, p. 129, Grierson to Gough, November 6, 1899.

[4] *Ibid.,* XIV, No. 3925, p. 405, Hatzfeldt to Hohenlohe, December 22, 1898.

[5] *Ibid.,* XIV, No. 3908, p. 388, Metternich to Richthofen, November 6, 1898.

[6] *Parliamentary Debates,* LX, 265.

geous desecration of the Mahdi's tomb" after the battle of Omderman.[7] During the debate on the army
estimates (February) John Morley reminded the government that two years before the Chancellor of the
Exchequer had said that "in the interests of England
I wish we were not in Egypt"; but now to add the
Sudan would be to incur greater liabilities.[8] Morley
then moved to loftier ground and deprecated the acqui-
sition of any dominions which could only be governed
by despotic rule, which in its turn would exercise a
baneful effect upon British democracy.[9] Another member observed ironically that "nothing succeeds like
success, especially military success; and if you can add
that the military success has been gained cheaply, you
have achieved the crowning glory."[10] Labouchere de-
rided the notion that new markets must be opened;
and he made the startling proposal that negotiations
with France should at once be opened on the basis of
the Wolff Convention—that is to say, of the evacuation of Egypt—and that the Sudan should be turned
over to Egypt.[11]

But the government had another view of imperial
necessities. Broderick retorted on the jeering allusions
to getting empire "on the cheap" by demonstrating
that, after all, this had been "the cheapest development
of Imperialism which the present century had seen."
Moreover, he did not think that Great Britain should
be too "squeamish" about despotic rule among races

[7] *Ibid.,* LXVI, 1455.

[8] *Ibid.,* LXVII, 461.   [10] *Ibid.,* LXVII, 482.

[9] *Ibid.,* LXVII, 464.   [11] *Ibid.,* LXVII, 505.

unfit for free institutions.[12] Some members of the opposition were of the same opinion. Sir Edward Grey also
argued that in the race for empire the pace had been
forced by their competitors, and that the chief justification for reconquest was that it was inevitable.[13]

Here, indeed, Sir Edward Grey had touched upon
real grounds for the government's policy. It was necessary to enter the Sudan, not because it would be a
cheap expansion, or would open new markets, or check
barbarism, but because Great Britain's place in Egypt
had been challenged by the French advance into the
upper Nile territories. The government refused to
look back once it had set its hand to the policy. It had
no intention of relinquishing either to barbarism or to
the French such territories—whether more or less—as
had been won for the empire. The memory of Gordon,
the new laurels of the army, the very railway lately
built across a wilderness were pledges against such
renunciation.

Moreover, Salisbury could not have retreated now
without risking his government. As matters stood even
the Liberals, again under the leadership of Rosebery,
would hardly have relented toward France. A member
of the House of Lords went so far as to maintain in the
hearing of Münster in Paris that had Rosebery been
prime minister war would certainly have broken out;
and that, indeed, Rosebery had won back his somewhat diminished popularity by his present warlike at-

[12] *Ibid.,* LXVII, 481.

[13] *Ibid.,* LXVII, 490–97.

titude.[14] Rumbold, the British ambassador in Vienna, told Count Goluchowski that England was resolved to fight rather than yield; that her belligerency was more than *Säbelrasseln*.[15] Naval preparations were still being zealously pushed forward, and it was said that in Plymouth and Portsmouth work was going on day and night.[16] Salisbury tried to minimize the significance of these activities by explaining that they had been determined upon during the previous spring—that is to say, before the difficulties with France had arisen.[17] But Chamberlain, on the other hand, had prophesied grimly, "You will see what is going to happen as soon as our war preparations are finished"—after Christmas, in January or February, no telling just when.[18]

Inasmuch as France had yielded in the matter of Fashoda, these preparations and alarms were disturbing to foreign observers, and not quite explicable. Could it mean that England was about to seek some other occasion against France? that the Lion lately blooded at Fashoda was now in a killing mood? In London demands were being heard for a British pro-

[14] *G.P.*, XIV, No. 3927, p. 410, Münster to Hohenlohe, January 6, 1899.

[15] *British Documents*, I, No. 231, p. 191, Rumbold to Salisbury, November 9.

[16] *G.P.*, XIV, No. 3927, p. 410, Münster to Hohenlohe, January 6, 1899.

[17] *Ibid.*, No. 3925, p. 406, Hatzfeldt to Hohenlohe, December 22, 1898; *Parliamentary Debates*, LXVIII, 315.

[18] *G.P.*, XIV, No. 3908, p. 388, Metternich to Richthofen, November 6, 1898.

tectorate in Egypt; and it was believed that Salisbury
was about to make a declaration in that sense. Was it
not possible, then, that Great Britain was preparing to settle out of hand that inveterate polemic, the
Egyptian question? The German ambassador in London thought not; he believed rather that the British
government was making provision against the moment when France would come forward with exorbi-
tant claims for compensation in the Bahr-el-Ghazelle
or elsewhere. And he was of opinion that while France
would hardly allow herself to be dragged into a war
for the sake of Fashoda alone, yet it was very doubtful
if she would endure *ruhiges Blut* to have England raise
and peremptorily settle the Egyptian question in her
own interests.[19]

On the side of France, meanwhile, feeling was apparently somewhat less aggressive. The Dreyfus case
had prostrated the country in a sort of moral debility.
There had been but lately rumors of a military plot in
Paris and of an intended coup d'état—although as yet
no "Boulanger" had emerged to give point and corrob-
oration to the gossip. The German ambassador pronounced France *chronisch sehr krank;* she had lost her
early patriotism, thought no more of *gloire,* hated
traitorous Jews, worshiped the golden calf, and was
fearful of war.[20] At Fashoda France had suffered de-

[19] *Ibid.,* XIV, No. 3909, p. 390, Rudenhausen to Hohenlohe,
November 8, 1898; No. 3910, p. 391, Müller to Foreign Office, November 9, 1898.

[20] *Ibid.,* XIII, No. 3618, p. 316, Münster to Hohenlohe, December 18, 1898.

feat without a struggle, and it was now doubly inglori-
ous that there seemed to be after all no safety in capit-
ulation. There was a painful conviction abroad that
Russia would not raise a finger in behalf of France;
and it was said that Count Muravieff had during the
crisis secretly advised yielding to England. The British seemed openly and insolently to count upon Russia's abstention. Great Britain's whole conduct filled
the French with suspicion and some fear. The publica-
tion in January of a British *Blue Book* on the Madagascar negotiations seemed to the French an entirely
needless affront. It touched them on the raw, and the
newspapers rose to a sharper note of resentment.[21]
President Faure regarded the situation as grave, especially since *son ami Nicolas* had failed him; and he
could only put his trust in Salisbury and Queen Victoria, who, he had convinced himself, were staunch for
peace.[22] There must have been besides a good deal of
dislocation and uneasiness even in private quarters.
English winter travelers did not invade the French re-
sorts as usual—were largely diverted to the Italian
Riviera. In the hotels at Cannes families were engaging quarters only on condition of no war with England.[23]

So much tension must have been growing almost

[21] *Ibid.,* XIV, No. 3928, p. 411, Münster to Hohenlohe, January 10, 1899.

[22] *Ibid.,* XIV, No. 3927, p. 409, Münster to Hohenlohe, January 3, 1899; No. 3928, p. 412.

[23] *Ibid.,* XIV, No. 3926, p. 408, Münster to Hohenlohe, December 29, 1898.

insupportable. Nothing was to be gained by prolonging it, and yet both sides seemed determined not to be
the first to break silence and enter upon a frank discussion of pending questions. It does seem, indeed, that
Great Britain, who had refused a discussion before
Fashoda, for whom Fashoda had been a definite triumph, and who presumably had now less to sacrifice
either in pride or in practical benefits by taking the
initiative in negotiation, could have at least dissem-
bled her irritation and come forward with proposals
for a settlement. Lord Salisbury may have been disposed to be magnanimous; he had a way of doing
things handsomely when treating with foreign powers
which sometimes deeply irritated the British jingoes;
and his known inclination in this instance to grant
France some compensation had already drawn upon
him from the Kaiser a bad-tempered epithet, "Der alte
Gallische Fuchs."[24] But Salisbury was no doubt em-
barrassed by the harsher attitude of some of his colleagues and by the inflamed public opinion. And besides France was standing very much on her dignity,
and was apparently unwilling to yield a tactical advantage by seeming to be more concerned over the situation than was her adversary. The French ambassador in London told the Russian ambassador that
France had no occasion to initiate negotiations over
outstanding questions; that there was no necessity for
France to compass a change in existing relations, and

[24] *Ibid.*, XIV, No. 3923, p. 403, marginal.

that she could content herself with them for some time longer.[25]

M. Cambon was putting a very good face on circumstances. But he was even then (January 12) in the very act of beginning conversations with Lord Salisbury which, it was hoped, would lead to a settlement.[26] There seems to have been at first a little mystery made over these negotiations, the other governments being kept a good deal in the dark. The day after their inception the Russian ambassador confessed himself unable to discover whether as yet any negotiations were under way; and Lord Salisbury, in receiving Hatzfeldt just after the departure of M. Cambon, made no mention of the previous interview, although he plainly showed some secret irritation.[27] Two weeks later Salisbury was still very reserved about the negotiations with France; he admitted only that in a general way they were treating, but had not got far.[28] None of the foreign representatives yet knew how matters prospered. Suspicions seem to have been aroused, therefore, that France and England were extending their bargaining beyond the immediate questions of central Africa. But in the beginning of February Hatzfeldt

[25] *Ibid.,* XIV, No. 3929, p. 413, Hatzfeldt to Hohenlohe, January 13, 1899.

[26] *British Documents,* I, No. 240, p. 197, Salisbury to Monson, January 11, 1899.

[27] *G.P.,* XIV, No. 3929, p. 413, Hatzfeldt to Hohenlohe, January 13, 1899.

[28] *Ibid.,* XIV, No. 3930, p. 414, Hatzfeldt to Hohenlohe, January 26, 1899.

was able to reassure his government on that score. He wrote home that there was no evidence that the Anglo-French negotiations had to do, as was feared, with a partition of the Spanish colonies.[29]

M. Cambon saw at the very outset of the discussions that the British government would oppose any political establishment by France on the upper Nile. The discovery could not have been a matter of much surprise. The French must have known well enough before they undertook to treat that the British would indubitably lay down as a preliminary postulate the complete evacuation of the Bahr-el-Ghazelle. It was not to be supposed that they would give now what they refused before the surrender of Fashoda. Cambon therefore gave his government the obviously good advice that if they wished to come to an agreement it would be well to confine themselves to seeking a trade-route to the upper Nile, and to assuring themselves a favorable delimitation of their zone of influence east of Lake Chad.[30]

As for a trade-route, however, if it involved French posts along its course—armed posts after all along the Bahr-el-Ghazelle—it was hardly to be thought of in England. But what Delcassé really proposed (February 10) was only freedom of trade both ways along certain avenues;[31] and on his part Salisbury was

[29] *Ibid.*, XIV, No. 3932, p. 415, Hatzfeldt to Foreign Office, February 2, 1899.

[30] *Documents Diplomatiques: Correspondance . . . . la déclaration additionelle (Dec. add.)*, No. 1, Cambon to Delcassé, January 12, 1899.

[31] *Ibid.*, No. 6, Delcassé to Cambon, February 10, 1899.

ready to concede an opening on the Nile, providing no territorial title were tied to the right.[32] Such privileges, however, were illusory in an untamed wilderness; and as it turned out the field of negotiation was soon reduced to the simple problem of delimitation.

Salisbury had informed his colleagues in the cabinet of the intention to proceed to the delimitation of zones of influence, and on January 21 he was able to report to Cambon that they had given the matter a quite favorable reception.[33] He then invited the French ambassador to propose a line of demarcation. Accordingly, Cambon suggested a line following in general the Nile-Congo watershed, and proceeding northward along the eastern frontiers of Wadai. France would thus be abandoning the whole of the Bahr-el-Ghazelle, but might in turn be compensated by a recognition of her authority in all the regions north and east of Lake Chad.[34] Salisbury made no immediate objections; later he accepted the project. And, indeed, this first scheme furnished the principle for the final definition.

Meanwhile and as might have been expected, the mere fact that diplomacy had again begun to function dissipated gradually the menace of war. A relaxation of tension was soon apparent and public opinion

[32] *G.P.,* XIV, No. 3933, p. 416, Hatzfeldt to Foreign Office, February 17, 1899.

[33] *Documents Diplomatiques: Correspondance concernant la déclaration additionelle du 21 Mars, 1899,* No. 3, Cambon to Delcassé, January 21, 1899.

[34] *Ibid.,* No. 3; *British Documents,* I, No. 244, p. 201, Salisbury to Monson, February 15, 1899.

on both sides grew more calm.[35] On the 13th of March Queen Victoria came to Nice. She was received respectfully and with military honors, although the populace was cold—no cheering.[36] And when on the fifteenth Salisbury confirmed the report that negotiations with France had taken a happy turn, peace seemed assured.[37]

On March 21 the two governments signed an agreement mutually promising to appoint commissioners charged with establishing a delimitation in conformity with an accompanying declaration.[38] Therein a line was laid out from a point where the French-Congolese boundary meets the Nile-Congo watershed, northward along the crest of that watershed to 11° North Latitude; thence it was to follow in general the old boundary of 1882 between Wadai and Darfur. The French government promised to acquire neither territory nor political influence east of that line, and the British government promised to acquire neither territory nor political influence west of it. The declaration was ratified three months later as a supplement of Article IV of the Anglo-French Convention of June 14, 1898, a convention which so far had failed of ratification.

Delcassé expressed immediately his relief and sat-

[35] *G.P.*, XIV, No. 3931, p. 415.

[36] *Ibid.*, XIV, No. 3940, p. 420, Münster to Bülow, March 13, 1899.

[37] *Ibid.*, XIV, No. 3942, p. 422, Hatzfeldt to Foreign Office, March 15, 1899.

[38] *British and Foreign State Papers*, XCI (1898–99), 55, text of agreement; *Archives Diplomatiques*, I, 210; *Parliamentary Papers: Egypt No. 2, 1899*.

isfaction over the agreement. It was just to both sides, he declared, and should leave neither of them embittered. He bore himself, Count Münster thought, as a man who had escaped a great danger.[39] In the Senate he rendered an eloquent and almost triumphant apologia. There was now, he said, a great deal of sand where the Gallic cock could scratch at his ease, while the Bahr-el-Ghazelle offered immense marshes where the British duck might rejoice in full liberty. And besides,

after Mr. Cecil Rhodes had pushed the British flag to the southern shores of Lake Tanganyika, when in the north successively Dongola, Berber, and Khartoum had been snatched from the Mahdists, what statesman who had not completely lost the sense of reality, what minister knowing that from Cairo in twenty days thousands of soldiers could be brought to the Bahr-el-Ghazelle by way of the Nile, while it would have taken the French a year to bring up a few hundred exhausted soldiers,—knowing this, who would have dared to ask of the country the useless sacrifice of blood and treasure by which one might have been able merely to try to dispute this territory?[40]

The convention could not, of course, escape the scrutiny, more or less hostile, of the other powers, no matter how satisfactory it might be to the principals.

It is probable that the Czar, at any rate, was gratified by the new agreement. During the crisis he had seemed almost to dissociate himself from his ally.

[39] *G.P.,* XIV, No. 4943–44, pp. 423–24, Münster to Hohenlohe, March 24, 1899.

[40] Stuart, *French Foreign Policy,* p. 31 (quotes *Annales du Sénat,* LIV, 830).

Whatever may have been his obligations under the French alliance, his recent passivity had certainly borne the appearance of a sort of disloyalty. It was an invidious position, and he now escaped it. As for the Kaiser, he expressed himself characteristically by jeering impartially at both parties to the agreement. On Münster's report that Delcassé was taking comfort in the thought that at last there had been removed a source of constant dissensions with England, the Emperor wrote, "Harmloser Mann! der kenne John Bull nicht"; and on the statement that Salisbury was happy to have silenced the jingoes, and that he had bound himself to avoid a European war during the Queen's lifetime, his comment was, "Cavalièrement gehandelt, aber sehr unpraktisch"—he has let slip a magnificent occasion.[41]

But there were two other powers who felt themselves intimately concerned in the Anglo-French agreement, and who vehemently protested its terms and its implications. These were Turkey and Italy.

The agreement had disposed summarily of the whole southern hinterland of Tripoli in the interests of France. At least that was the implication in the promise made by Great Britain not to extend her own influence into those regions. But Tripoli was a province of the Turkish Empire, the last (if Egypt be excepted) of its once magnificent territories in North Africa. The Porte was growing justifiably apprehensive and touchy over its outlying possessions. The for-

[41] *G.P.*, XIV, No. 3944, p. 425, marginal.

eign minister, Tewfik Pasha, did not "protest" the agreement, but he told the German ambassador (April 1) that he had made reservations in London and Paris. The English reply was slow in coming; but Delcassé had told the Turkish ambassador that the lands assigned to France under the convention had been unoccupied, and that therefore no one possessed rights in them. It was a fresh application of the useful doctrine of *res nullius*. But Tewfik Pasha was unconvinced, and complained to Von Marschall of this infringement of the special provisions of the treaty of Berlin, appealing to him also on the ground that all powers with possessions on Lake Chad (and therefore Germany, too) should interest themselves in the question. Since France was everywhere notoriously hostile to foreign trade, the Lake Chad lands, he was sure, would be enveloped and cut off from their Mediterranean outlets.[42] When at last the British reply arrived it was to the effect that Italy and France were entering into direct negotiations over the question of Tripoli's hinterland. Again Tewfik Pasha was not satisfied, as, indeed, how should he be? It was Turkey, not Italy, which was primarily touched.[43] For Italy to treat with another power concerning the hinterland of a Turkish province must have seemed a piece of insolent presumption.

[42] *Ibid.,* XIV, No. 3949, pp. 431–32, Marschall to Foreign Office, April 1, 1899; *British Documents,* I, No. 253, p. 208; Anthopoulo Pasha to Salisbury.

[43] *G.P.,* XIV, No. 3951, p. 433, Marschall to Foreign Office, April 13, 1899; *British Documents,* I, No. 254, p. 209, Salisbury to Anthopoulo Pasha.

Later (June 3) Salisbury, wishing to reinstate him-self with the Turkish government, disclaimed any in-tended offense toward Turkey. So far as England was concerned, he said, nothing was changed in the Tripol-itan hinterland; England had expressly pledged her-self not to expand into those territories. He therefore referred the Porte to France.[44] Nothing, apparently, was to be got by pursuing the matter further; here therefore was an occasion for the simple exercise of oriental resignation.

In Italy's case also the ground of discontent with the Anglo-French agreement was that it allotted to the French sphere all lands between Lake Chad and the Tripolitan frontier—wherever that might be. Italy had not yet made formal claims to the reversion of Tripoli, but she "could not remain indifferent" to its fate—had not been indifferent for the past twenty years. The Anglo-French agreement, therefore, threw the Italian government into a state of consternation.

Italy had always regarded England as one of her liberators. And there was, indeed, no doubt of the great moral services rendered by England to Italy thirty-five years before. France, who had actually drawn the sword in behalf of Italian unity, had subse-quently forfeited the gratitude she earned. But Eng-land still enjoyed in 1898 the fruits of her ancient good will and disinterestedness. Only a few years be-fore (1891) at the renewal of the Triple Alliance, It-aly had wished to have included in the treaty, as in the

[44] *G.P.*, XIV, No. 3957, p. 437, Marschall to Foreign Office, June 3, 1899.

protocol of 1882, the clause declaring the treaty not directed against England.[45] England was, of course, ignorant of this evidence of the survival of Italian good feeling toward herself. Nevertheless she knew that Italy esteemed her as a friend and almost as a patron; that Italy seemed, indeed, to fasten her hopes as much upon England's good graces in North Africa as upon those of her partners in the Triple Alliance who had also pledged their support in those territories.[46] In the Mediterranean agreements of 1887 Italy had declared herself "entirely ready to support the work of Great Britain in Egypt," and Great Britain had promised to "support the action of Italy at every other point whatsoever of the North African coast districts, and especially in Tripolitania and Cyrenaica."[47]

Moreover, as regards the Sudan specifically, Italy and Great Britain had gone easily hand in hand. For Great Britain, being anxious to block French penetration toward the Nile from the east, had encouraged Italy in her pretensions to a protectorate in Abyssinia.[48] But Italy's resources had not been equal to her ambitions. And when on March 1, 1896, Baratieri's army was annihilated by Menelik's levies, Italy was forced to recognize Abyssinia's "absolute inde-

[45] Pribram, *The Secret Treaties of Austria-Hungary, 1879–1914,* I, 69. *Additional Declaration,* 1882; Lowes-Dickinson, *The International Anarchy, 1904–1914,* p. 93.

[46] Pribram, *op. cit.,* I, 157.

[47] *Ibid.,* I, 96–97.

[48] Débidour, *Histoire diplomatique,* I, 196.

pendence without reservation,"[49] an almost unique
check to the European penetration of Africa. Great
Britain felt impelled, perhaps, to do something for her
protégé; and her sudden plunge three months later
into the reconquest of the Sudan may have been taken
partly as a diversion to relieve Italy.

Great Britain and Italy having become each an
accomplice of the other in Africa, it is not surprising
that the Italian government was filled with bitter dismay over the Anglo-French agreement of March 21,
1899. Had not England herself given confidential assurances that Italy might take over the administration of Tripoli in case it were lost to Turkey? When,
some months before, disquieting rumors had come to
the knowledge of the Italian foreign minister, had not
Lord Cromer put him off and silenced him by a specific denial? This concealment was perfidy. The Italian government was anxious, declared the foreign minister to the German ambassador at Rome, to maintain
good relations with England—in the interests, of
course, of the Triple Alliance—but he owned that he
was not clear how it was to be done. He would be
pleased to learn from the Imperial German government what they thought of this infringement of the
status quo in the Mediterranean; which also, it should
be said, had the appearance of a triumph of French
policy at the expense of one of the states of the Triple
Alliance. The foreign minister ventured to hope that
the Imperial government would undertake an effective

[40] Ferry, *L'Ethiopie,* pp. 20–23.

intervention in the matter of the Anglo-French agreement.[50]

As a matter of fact, however, the German government contented itself with delivering a note through Hatzfeldt in London reserving German rights in Africa. But to assuage Italy's indignation and to meet somehow her importunities, the German and Austrian governments gave the Italian foreign minister (Canevaro) permission to state, in reply to interpellations in Parliament, that those powers approved the attitude of Italy.[51] With these condescensions Italy had to content herself on the side of her allies; and from France she had no more than polite assurances that Italy's designs in Tripoli would not be opposed.[52] Italy, therefore, like Turkey, succumbed to the inevitable.

Here must end the narrative account of the collisions in Africa and the diplomatic disputes in Europe which together constituted the Fashoda incident. These matters are intelligible enough in themselves, given, that is, two rival and imperialistic powers for whom the world seemed all too small. But it is quite possible to have understood the points of the controversy, and perhaps to have struck a just balance between the conflicting arguments, and yet to find the outcome incomprehensible. A most careful study of

[50] *G.P.*, XIV, Nos. 3946–48, pp. 429–31; *British Documents*, I, Nos. 246–49, pp. 203–6.

[51] *G.P.*, XIV, Nos. 3954–56, pp. 436–37.

[52] *Ibid.*, XIV, No. 3953, p. 435, Saurma to Foreign Office, April 28, 1899.

the correspondence between Paris and London will not reveal the causes of the French renunciation. For who shall say that on the face of it Delcassé's case did not have merit? We may dismiss at once, therefore, the idea that he had at last found justice and reasonableness in the British claims; for he had himself already assaulted and breached at too many points the logic of the position taken by Great Britain. It was certainly not Lord Salisbury's skill in dialectic which vanquished him. There remains, therefore, an even more interesting inquiry, namely into the ultimate circumstances which determined Delcassé's decision.

PART II
THE DIPLOMATIC SETTING

CHAPTER VII

MOTIVES OF THE FRENCH RENUNCIATION

It would be difficult to discover all the promptings and calculations which moved the French government to abandon Fashoda. There were, however, certain considerations which must have presented themselves with a good deal of weight.

And first, it was a question whether for France the possession of Fashoda was worth a European war of the first magnitude. In itself the province of the Bahr-el-Ghazelle could not have been of much immediate value to either party to the dispute. Its eastern half was indeed generally "a miserable swampy bog," with a climate notoriously deadly to white men. And whatever its resources in lands or mines might ultimately prove to be, they must inevitably lie unused for a long time, "like the gold hid in a peasant's stocking."[1] These were, almost literally, "annexations in the Mountains of the Moon."[2]

Moreover, it is not likely that France could have derived any vital advantage from the geographical position of these territories. Their possession would not have particularly enhanced the value of French holdings farther west. An open door on the Nile would not

[1] L. Decle, "Fashoda Question," *Fortnightly Rev.,* LXIV (November, 1898), 669.

[2] *British Documents,* I, No. 208, p. 178, Monson to Salisbury, October 10.

have served the French Ubangi country nearly so well as did the Congo outlet. De Brazza had declared that France had "an indisputable right to use freely a means of transit of as great general importance as the Congo waterway."[3] But in the Bahr-el-Ghazelle province that means of transit does not exist for ten months in the year. The Anglo-Egyptian steamers now plying on the Sueh are able to reach Wau only between the middle of July and the middle of September.[4]

No natural boundaries would have been achieved by occupying the banks of the Nile, no convenient rounding out of territory. The Bahr-el-Ghazelle lay apart and utterly remote; it would have been an almost indefensible outwork, rashly tempting capture. Neither could it very well have served as the first instalment in a new belt of French empire extending eastward and linking the Congo with the Indian Ocean. The execution of any such grand design would have been enormously difficult. For from the headwaters of the Congo eastward there is no clear thoroughfare across Africa. Had the French not been stopped at the Nile, they might very well have been stopped at the foot of the Abyssinian plateau, even assuming that they would have had to contend only with natural obstacles. And while they prosecuted their adventure eastward they would have had to feed and clothe and arm themselves with what they could carry up the Congo from the west. "En Afrique," writes Hanotaux, "les fleuves ne viennent pas en aide à la civilisa-

[3] *Times,* October 3.

[4] *Sudan Almanac* (1923), p. 31.

tion; ils l'entravent."[5] The Congo would have been but
a primitive, slender, and expensive line of transport;
and it was then costing £500 a ton to bring goods from
the west coast.[6]

It seems, therefore, that there would have been
little wisdom in plunging France into a great war for
so dubious and modest a stake—for commercial and
political advantages as yet undeveloped and only con-
jectural.

The war, besides, would not have been on equal
terms; for France was a land power, and would have
been under grave disabilities in a transmarine and colonial war. The French minister of marine had drawn
up comprehensive building plans, for which in December he wished the consent of Parliament.[7] But in general France was unprepared for a war of the sort
Great Britain would wage; and to have asked the
Chambre for credits to remedy her case in that ultimate moment would have been to precipitate the conflict. As for the new submarine torpedo-boat which the
French had devised, Hatzfeldt in London pronounced
it a plaything; the French were children, he thought,
putting their trust in a novelty, as in '70 they had
trusted in the mitrailleuse.[8] Moreover, France was
plainly out of heart at the prospect of war. The late

[5] Hanotaux, *Fachoda,* p. 21.

[6] Decle, *loc. cit.*

[7] *Grosse Politik,* XIV, No. 3926, p. 407, Münster to Hohenlohe, December 29, 1898.

[8] *Ibid.,* XIV, No. 3931, p. 415, Münster to Foreign Office,
January 31, 1899.

Spanish-American war had given a demonstration which was not to be ignored of the terrible efficacy of sea-power. And in France the conviction was being openly expressed that if it came to fighting, England could sink the entire French navy in two weeks—that she could do it and that she wished to do it.[9] In case of war the whole intention seemed to be to defend the coasts, nothing more; a course which in the opinion of the German emperor amounted to abdication on the seas.[10]

In very striking contrast was Britain's confidence in her naval superiority and readiness. During the October crisis, when feeling in England had risen to the bubble, there were rumors and newspaper reports of activities at Portsmouth. The German naval attaché judged that all preparations were so far advanced that it required only the order for mobilization to complete them.[11] It will be remembered that Lord Salisbury denied that the government was undertaking special measures of defense. If there seemed to be unusual activity in the yards at Plymouth and elsewhere, it had been occasioned by the Fashoda incident only, he said, in the sense that the navy had to coal and otherwise prepare for any eventuality. And he added jestingly that if Goschen were really making other preparations, he must be engaging in them secretly

[9] *Ibid.,* XIII, No. 3558, p. 250, Huhn of *Kölnische Zeitung.*

[10] *Ibid.,* XIV, No. 3926, p. 409, marginal.

[11] *Ibid.,* XIV, No. 3898, p. 381, German Naval attaché in London, October 25, 1898.

and in the privacy of his own room, for he himself was not informed of them.[12]

But special measures were not actually needed to insure an almost certain naval superiority over the French, provided, at least, that they were to be met alone and not in coalition. Since 1894–95 Great Britain had increased her naval forces by 27,000 men,[13] and had been spending five times as much as France for her navy. British sea-power was not then disputed, nor likely to be disputed for some time to come. In a dispatch to Hatzfeldt earlier in the year, Bülow had written that in the unanimous opinion of German naval officers, and among them Admiral Tirpitz, the English fleet was easily without a rival.[14] England herself was aware of this superiority. Chamberlain had once boasted to the German ambassador that there was no need to flinch for a moment from a duel with France. He admitted that it might be another matter to contend against the whole strength of France and Russia combined.[15] But during the summer of 1898 the Russian naval maneuvers had made a bad impression;[16] and now the Russian ships, laid up for the winter in

[12] *Ibid.*, XIV, No. 3925, p. 406, Hatzfeldt to Hohenlohe, December 22, 1898.

[13] *Parliamentary Debates,* LXVIII, 315.

[14] *G.P.,* XIV, No. 3783, p. 201, Bülow to Hatzfeldt, March 30, 1898.

[15] *Ibid.*, XIV, No. 3784, p. 203, Hatzfeldt to Foreign Office, April 1, 1898.

[16] *Ibid.*, XIV, No. 3909, p. 390, Rudenhausen to Hohenlohe, November 8, 1898.

their frozen harbors, would be even less effective than those of France. And in any case, as it turned out later, and as it might even then have been surmised, the Russian navy was not at the disposal of France.

In a conflict with France at that moment, therefore, the greater risks were admittedly not on the side of Great Britain. And Lord Salisbury need not, and there is no reason to suppose that he would, have drawn back from a contemplation of war. It may even have crossed his mind that the moment was not unfavorable for permanently disabling a dangerous rival. Indeed, that view of the situation was commonly imputed to some of his colleagues in government.[17] Goschen and Chamberlain particularly were supposed to be resolved upon another and decisive "Trafalgar." The German emperor seems to have been convinced, even against argument, that England actually intended to make war; and he judged that "from the military point of view, the moment was well chosen."[18] And certainly the French were persuaded that Great Britain harbored the most dishonest and unscrupulous designs against themselves; and the knowledge of their own weakness and isolation must have lent weight to these apprehensions. They seemed convinced that if the war party in England should actually prevail, then France would be exposed to the most desperate haz-

[17] *Ibid.*, XIV, No. 3898, p. 381, report of German naval attaché in London, October 25, 1898; *British Documents*, I, No. 241, p. 199, Monson to Salisbury, January 13, 1899.

[18] *Ibid.*, I, No. 124, p. 103, Lascelles to Salisbury, December 21, 1898.

ards. It is notable that the martial temper of the nation did not this time leap up with its wonted *élan.*

Moreover, the British government had a great advantage over their adversaries in Paris in being wholly unencumbered in domestic politics. Salisbury's government was secure among the constituencies; and on this particular point of foreign policy there can be no doubt that the whole weight of public opinion in England was against compromise. The supporters of drastic measures toward France were zealous and very outspoken. The German naval attaché in London had heard from private individuals such expressions as that "we will thrash the French, and then take from them Tunis and whatever else we want."[19] Members of government like Chamberlain, and Devonshire, and Goschen, wherein they differed from their chief, differed in the direction of advocating harder dealings. They were supposed to regard the moment as favorable for a final reckoning with France, and Chamberlain had expressed himself in almost those terms. It is not, indeed, likely that Salisbury would have so far abdicated as to allow his policy to be forced by his political subordinates. But he must have rested secure in the knowledge that he could proceed as far as he liked against France without serious danger of domestic opposition.

The negotiators in Paris were in not nearly so comfortable a posture. There they labored among distractions unknown to the Salisbury government. Home politics had to be conducted on a basis of im-

[19] *G.P.,* XIV, No. 3898, p. 381.

permanent arrangements among the shifting factions of the Chambre. And without an adequate party discipline the French ministers could not at any time rely upon a dignified security of power. At the very peak of the Fashoda crisis the Brisson cabinet had fallen (October 26), not indeed from failure to give satisfaction in its foreign policy, but nevertheless to the great damage of the pending negotiations with Great Britain. Delcassé might well have profited personally by the change of ministry. By leaving office with his colleagues he might have escaped the odium of responsibility for capituation to British demands. He clearly showed his reluctance to join the new Dupuy cabinet, and he made it plain that his reasons were that he was unwilling to give the order for the unconditional evacuation of Fashoda, a step which then began to appear inevitable. "It is you," he told the British ambassador, "who make it impossible for me to remain," i.e., in office.[20] Nevertheless and in the end he did remain to play a distasteful part at the Quay d'Orsay in the ministry of Dupuy.

At that moment, too, the normal difficulties of government were aggravated by unusual domestic ferments. The notorious Dreyfus case had been lately reopened, and public sentiment was fevered to a pitch of passion now scarcely intelligible. Militarists, monarchists, nationalists, and anti-Semites made a bitter political controversy out of what should have been a

[20] *Ibid.*, XIV, No. 3901, p. 383, Münster to Foreign Office, October 29, 1898; *British Documents,* I, No. 221, p. 184, Monson to Salisbury, October 28.

sober judicial proceeding. France was weakened almost as if by a civil war. Humiliating revelations of perjury and forgery had touched the honor of the army, and French military pride had lost some of its hardihood. Delcassé's foreign policy could not possibly have ignored or risen above these protracted and disreputable turmoils. "England has her hands free," declared the *Cologne Gazette*, "while the energies of France are paralyzed by the Dreyfus case."[21] In the army there was demoralization, among the masses the authority of government was being undermined, and everywhere there was apathy and enervation. The republic itself seemed no longer secure, and the republican leaders were ready for any expedient, however unworthy (so it was said), to avoid a crisis and remain at the helm.[22] In October there were sensational rumors of a conspiracy of the military against Brisson. Münster, the German ambassador, did not credit what he heard because, as he pointed out, in a special report to Bülow, for a revolution there must be revolutionaries, and there were very few such in Paris; while for a coup d'état there must be a man of energy with a following, and none had yet appeared. France was, nevertheless, in a very bad way indeed, he thought, although not yet ripe for revolution.[23] And later in the winter he arrived at the dismal conclusion that the republic must sink yet deeper before anything else could

[21] *Times*, September 28, 1898.

[22] *G.P.*, XIII, No. 3561, p. 255, Münster to Hohenlohe, February 4, 1899.

[23] *Ibid.*, XIII, Nos, 3612, 3615, 3618, pp. 310–16.

take its place.[24] Frenchmen as well as foreigners were losing hope that France could long escape internal convulsion; they talked of the corruption and cynicism, of the general rottenness of the state. There were gloomy forebodings on all sides.[25]

It was among these depressing circumstances that Delcassé was called upon to conduct the Fashoda negotiations. It was admirable that he should have displayed any resolution at all in foreign affairs, and he must be absolved, therefore, of too easily abandoning a cause. He had skirted the very precipice of war when, under the circumstances recited above, a retreat betimes might have been more prudent and not less honorable.

But and indeed it was not considerations of the internal weakness of France, or of the military odds against her, or of the doubtful value of the prospective prize in African territory, which would have most restrained Delcassé. These were but minor deterrents. He had another and exceedingly formidable reason for desisting in the unequal struggle, namely the precarious position of France in Europe. For France had liabilities quite outside her immediate dispute with England, which, however irrelevant, would be inevitably and overwhelmingly decisive in settling that particular score. In an issue like that of Fashoda both friends and enemies alike would find their occasions for profiting as they could from the necessities of the dispu-

[24] *Ibid.,* XIII, No. 3561, p. 256, Münster to Hohenlohe, February 4, 1899.

[25] *British Documents,* I, No. 172, p. 146, Monson to Salisbury, February 26, 1899.

tants. Politics was a wolfish game, and there were few
questions in Europe which could be settled on their
own merits. Delcassé had to have regard, therefore,
not only to France and England but to the rest of Europe besides; and it must have been these contingent
considerations which would weigh most heavily in his
calculations.

For that matter and similarly, it is probable that
Lord Salisbury, too, was least moved by what he may
have regarded as the favorable chances in a war with
France. To contemplate war was to contemplate desperate expedients, and it was notorious that in foreign
affairs Lord Salisbury was moderate and guarded. It
was not in foreign affairs that he had committed his
"blazing indiscretions"; there he had always kept
within lines of prudence and safety, had developed a
habit of "intelligent inaction," of "maintaining things
as they are."[26] But war is a rude disturber of things
as they are, and the evidence is plentiful that Lord
Salisbury was not, in the present instance, giving ear
to the incitements of his colleagues, nor putting his
trust in a presumptive victory over the French. On
the contrary, his reliance was still in diplomacy. And
if he now showed unwonted pertinacity, it must have
been rather because he felt confidence in his general
diplomatic posture.

Here, then, is the core of our inquiry: What influence, either known or inferred, did the general European situation have upon the final decisions taken by
the principals in the Fashoda dispute?

[26] *Cambridge History of British Foreign Policy,* III, 260.

The occupation of Fashoda was not specifically, of course, a matter of much interest to Europe outside of France and Great Britain. Neither of these two powers had been at any particular trouble to engage European sentiment in favor of its own peculiar pretensions in the Bahr-el-Ghazelle. Britain had relied upon her prescriptive position in the lower Nile Valley to justify in the eyes of Europe her advance into the hinterland. And France, working secretly, was precluded from negotiating openly and beforehand for a recognition of her claims. Nevertheless the European situation overshadowed the world; and nothing could be done whether in Africa or Asia that was not conditioned by affairs in Europe. Indeed, Monson, the British ambassador in Paris, seems at first to have half-expected that one at least of the European governments would intervene and assume the right to submit the Anglo-French controversy, as an offshoot of the general Eastern question, to the deliberation of the powers. And Delcassé also may have reflected, perhaps hopefully, upon this same contingency.[27] In any case, if France and Great Britain were even to think of going to war with each other over Fashoda they had first to look to the attitude of their neighbors; and for France it was even more rigorously necessary than for Great Britain.

England had somewhat withdrawn from Continental politics. Her position of isolation was not always "splendid," it is true; there had been moments when it

[27] *British Documents,* I, No. 204, p. 176, Monson to Salisbury, October 7.

amounted to friendlessness, and she had endured many small slights from those with whom she professed to be on good terms.[28] Nevertheless, she formed a sort of third party of her own between the two balanced alliances of the Continent. And it was a position not without advantages in liberty of action, since she was not formally committed to any treaty-allies whatever, nor in much danger of incurring the active hostility of both parties at once.

Not so France. France was involved inextricably in that precarious equilibrium of enmities called "the European balance of power." She was at the same time confronted by an inveterate foe and bound to an indispensable friend. Under constraint of these circumstances she had to be forever guarded in her actions, lest she somehow jar the European equipoise. Circumspection was almost a condition of her existence.

For almost a decade after the Franco-German war of 1870 France was too much prostrated to indulge in an active foreign policy. It was a dismal period of eclipse and self-effacement, an era of unstable authority at home and of impotence and lost prestige abroad. The national energies seemed to be in abeyance, and in foreign affairs France seemed to have no choice but to follow "that habit of middling actions which we call common-sense."

In 1879, however, after the election of Jules Grévy to succeed MacMahon, the Republicans won complete control of the government. The nation seemed to re-

[28] Grey, *Twenty-five Years,* Vol. I, chap. ii.

vive. And the new vitality brought with it a sense of dignity and worth which, in turn, was bound to express itself in tones of greater authority and assertiveness in foreign affairs. In those years France found herself confronted by a European situation in which the pre-eminence of Germany seemed to be the central and incontrovertible fact; and it was a pre-eminence which bore with particular weight upon France herself. The Republicans were not disposed to kiss the rod of 1870, but neither were they rash enough to put France in the way of a new humiliation. Like all patriotic Frenchmen they hoped, no doubt, to see justice done some day for the rape of Alsace-Lorraine. But they desired most of all the reinstatement of France as a great power. That was the spirit of *revanche* in its wider sense, and for that they were willing to postpone *revanche* in its literal sense of retribution. They set themselves, therefore, to avoid provocation for the present while they reserved the future and waited upon fortune. And, meanwhile, in order to make France great as she had once been great, the Republicans found a new outlet for her reviving ambitions and energies, namely colonial expansion. In Europe they remained as prudent and reserved as their predecessors under MacMahon; outside of Europe they began to show resolution and initiative.[29]

Germany was not, in the beginning at least, particularly hostile to French colonial expansion. When, for example, France occupied Tunis it was with the consent if not at the instigation of Bismarck himself,

[29] Schefer, *D'une guerre à l'autre*, pp. 64–67.

who hoped that Africa would serve as a sort of light-
ning conductor to deflect from Europe the restless
energies of the French.[30] And again in 1884, while
France was pressing her fortunes on the Niger and the
Congo, Bismarck having suddenly made up his mind
to take a hand in the game of African colonization,
was not above playing for a time in collusion with
France against England.

But these instances of mutual relenting and accommodation in Africa did not deeply alter the relations of the two powers in Europe. The Peace of
Frankfort, which remained only a sort of protracted
truce, stood between them. In France the policy of
revanche was only relaxed and adjourned, not abandoned. And if France could not bring herself to accept
definitively the military verdict of 1870, if she looked
forward to reversing it, then she was under necessity
of unremitting vigilance. She could not at any time
abandon herself completely to distant adventures
while at home perils hung ominously along her frontiers. The truth was that colonies and *revanche* were
scarcely compatible; and an extreme prudence would
have regarded them as alternatives. But, for better or
for worse, France was committed to both at once.

The balance was not always kept even, however,
between the two simultaneous policies. The necessities of one were usually met at the expense of the other.
A pushing colonial policy required the propitiation of
Germany; and a stiff policy toward Germany meant
neglect of the colonies. Frenchmen were by no means

[30] Rose, *The Development of the European Nations,* II, 14.

agreed where the emphasis should rest. Therefore, first one and then the other principle was the more considered, and French policy was broken into periods more or less marked by these preferences. In the eighteen years preceding the rise of the Fashoda issue, it is possible to mark off three such periods: the first, under the inspiration of Ferry, regarded chiefly the colonies and good relations with Germany; the last, under the inspiration of Hanotaux, faced the same way; and between them lay an interval of seven or eight years of strained relations with Germany and a notable diminution of colonial activity.

Opposition to expansion was still strong in France during the early eighties. Colonies were thought to be an expensive luxury like "a loge at the opera," the occupation of Tunis was regarded as a "national peril," and the French colonial policy as a diabolical invention of Bismarck.[31] In 1882 the failure of France to participate with England in the occupation of Egypt was largely due to a temporary triumph of the principle of *revanche* over that of expansion. In a great speech in the Chambre Clémenceau denounced intervention in Egypt. He called upon the government to avoid encumbrances. All Europe is covered with soldiers, he cried, therefore "réservez la liberté d'action de la France."

But with the rise of the influence of Ferry, and especially during the two years of 1884 and 1885, colonies had become the preoccupation of France. The

[31] D. Pasquet, "Comment la France a perdu l'Egypte," *Revue historique,* CVI, 48.

complement of Ferry's colonial policy was naturally conciliation toward Germany; and it was by a happy chance that in these same years Bismarck became involved in Africa, and found it convenient to associate himself with France. Ferry tried to walk the narrow middle ground of friendliness without intimacy. As regards Africa, he permitted himself to be associated with Bismarck at the general council board of the Concert of Europe, but skilfully avoided being closeted alone with him within a tight Franco-German special agreement. His course seemed to be vindicated by events; for at the Conference of Berlin France was generally supported by Germany in the frequent lively disagreements between France and England.[32]

But public opinion in France was puzzled and perplexed by the subtleties of Ferry's diplomacy. Devious courses are bewildering to the uninitiated, and the public scarcely knew and had not yet learned to much care about the colonial necessities which prompted their government's policy. The ministry which would traffic with the arch-enemy was guilty of a sort of treason. There was a bigotry of *revanche* which would not tolerate even the spirit of truce and accommodation which was all that could then be charged against Ferry.[33]

Ferry's fall (1885) brought about a rupture of the provisional entente with Germany. His successor at the Quay d'Orsay, Charles de Freycinet, accepted

[32] Débidour, I, 89–91.

[33] Débidour, *op. cit.*, I, 94; Barclay, *Thirty Years Anglo-French Reminiscences,* p. 90.

the public mandate that there should be no more ambiguous dealings in that direction. His foreign policy devoted itself rather to securing France in Europe by conciliating England and Russia. He declined Bismarck's overtures during the Anglo-Russian difficulties in 1885; he did not press the Egyptian conflict with England; and he supported Russia in the Balkan negotiations of the moment.[34] France thus reverted once more to the policy of biding her time. But if the risks were fewer, so also were the rewards. Bismarck wearied of making advances, and turned instead to England to help him in Africa. Once, indeed, de Freycinet tried ingratiation with Germany. In 1886 Herbette made a formal proposal in Berlin to Count Herbert Bismarck that Germany should join France in expelling England from Egypt. "The English were abominated in France," he said, "more than the Germans had ever been."[35] But Count Bismarck was unsympathetic. And from that time until well into the nineties French colonial achievements were essentially negative; while *revanche*, beginning at last to hope for a Russian alliance, waited smoldering, blazed once in the extravagances of Boulangism, and smoldered again.

Thus we arrive at the era of Hanotaux, the immediate predecessor of Delcassé, who was also the real promoter of the Marchand mission and the responsible author of the Fashoda incident. Hanotaux was the true successor of Ferry. Like Ferry, he deliberately

[34] Schefer, *op. cit.*, p. 134.

[35] *Cambridge History of British Foreign Policy,* III, 245.

entered upon a policy of expansion which brought him into conflict with British interests; and, like Ferry, he sought to gloss over and abate the ancient feud with Germany in order to win for himself a free hand against Great Britain.

Throughout the eighties and into the nineties, therefore, the rule seems to have been invariable that a policy of colonial expansion meant a policy of conciliation toward Germany; and, conversely, when conciliation was neglected expansion suffered a check. Indeed, upon a priori grounds alone it seems that one of these policies should have carried the other; the facts of history appear to confirm that conclusion.

The events sketched above concern us here, of course, only as they exemplify the generalization that France had two policies which she attempted to pursue simultaneously but which were essentially in conflict and which, in spite of her best endeavors, she could not bring into perfect harmony.

British foreign policy, on the other hand, had long had an admirable simplicity and singleness of purpose, the whole of which was maintenance of the empire. Until the ninth decade of the nineteenth century, that had been a comparatively easy task. The expansive forces of the industrial revolution had begun to operate earlier in England than elsewhere. British commerce had dilated slowly over the globe, and with it had waxed the British empire, not, indeed, after the disturbing, purposeful, pushing manner of later imperialism, but by casual and dilatory acts of the Colonial Office. Great Britain was simply releasing her own compressed energies into the voids of Africa and Asia. It was generally an easy and almost effortless expansion. There were no early rivalries. Of all the European powers of the first rank Great Britain alone possessed and was steadily enlarging an already considerable transmarine empire.

Under those circumstances British colonial interests would not have been much advanced by alliances in Europe. So long as Continental politics did not touch upon the sole object of Great Britain's policy she was content to stand aloof. Ever since she had extricated herself from the entanglements of the Napoleonic wars, and except for engagements with a temporary and specific object, she had maintained a detachment, due partly, of course, to her geographic position but also and especially to her preoccupation outside of Europe. Even the Continental balance of power over which she watched so anxiously was a thing especially to be desired when it left her out. Isolation was, therefore, England's natural and obvious estate. Colonies and isolation were complementary policies. Or perhaps it could be held that isolation was not a policy at all, but rather the consequence of a policy.

In the eighties, however, conditions changed sharply. In that decade, and particularly in Africa, other European powers began to invade the vast and solitary preserves of British enterprise. It was then that France, in a burst of returning energy, blocked out her stupendous north and west African empire, made good her hold on Madagascar, and took up a strong position on the Red Sea. It was then that Bismarck issued a *quo warranto* against England's pretensions in southwest Africa, and with the least possible compunction forced her to confirm him in the possession of enormous territories in east Africa as well. It was then that Belgium, in the person of her king, appropriated almost the whole prodigious extent of the Congo basin; and that Italy, bitterly lamenting her meager opportunities, found dubious consolation in Eritrea and Somaliland. Great Britain's rivals set her a killing pace throughout the eighties and on into the nineties; and it was during those years that the inconveniences of isolation became fully apparent.

As with other powers, so with Germany, England had kept an attitude of reserve more or less friendly. But under stress of mounting rivalries she began to cast about for sure friends in Europe; and quite naturally she turned first to Germany. But her tardy advances were only in apparent contradiction of her traditional policy. Her motives were, as ever, to be found in a regard for colonial rather than European interests; and that fact may partly explain her eventual failure to interest Germany in her proposals.

But if England, like France, was impelled by her colonial policy to fraternize with Germany there was yet this deep and significant difference: French colonial policy was always encumbered by a French European policy; England had only her habit of isolation from Europe, which resembled a negation of policy and implied no obligations. England needed only to content Germany outside of Europe, while France had also to propitiate her in Europe. And this double burden toward Germany might conceivably put France under a decisive disability in any serious colonial disagreement with England. In any case Germany would hold a very commanding position between the rivals.

The foregoing digressions (they are frankly that) are intended to prepare the way for an exposition of French and English policies during the Fashoda crisis. Perhaps the sketch has been too slight to be convincing. But it should have done something at least toward showing that France had always a double orientation of policy, while England had a single orientation of policy; that France pursued both colonies and *revanche*, while England pursued only colonies. Perhaps in what follows that observed principle may be more fully exemplified in the Fashoda incident, and the Fashoda incident be explained by the principle. It is necessary now to return to the more immediate diplomatic antecedents of the situation of 1898–99, and to examine what then occurred.

CHAPTER VIII

GERMANY AND THE DISPUTANTS

In April of 1898 the German Emperor sent to the British ambassador in Berlin a telegram of congratulation upon Kitchener's victory at the Atbara. At Hanover he harangued the troops and called for three cheers for the Queen.[1] On the other hand, in November he wrote to the Czar from Damascus deprecating the French surrender of Fashoda: "What on earth has possessed them?! After such a first rate well arranged and plucky expedition of poor and brave Marchand? They were in a first rate position and able to help us others all in Africa who are in need of strong help!"[2]

Where, then, lay the Kaiser's sympathies? With the venerable queen his grandmother? Or with the French who might have helped the "others all in Africa"? Or perhaps with neither?

One of the obvious advantages of Great Britain's detached position in Europe was that she need not, in fact could not, incur the open hostility of both opposing alliances simultaneously. To be having difficulties with a member of the Dual Alliance was presumptive of at least neutrality from the members of the Triple Alliance. By regarding only this general considera-

---

[1] J. Rennel Rodd, *Social and Diplomatic Memories,* Second Series, p. 210; Sir Sidney Lee, *King Edward,* I, 740.

[2] *Kaiser's Letters,* XVIII, 69.

tion there was no reason to expect that Germany would intervene in behalf of France.

Moreover, from the early eighties, that is to say from the beginnings of Bismarck's system of alliances, England had plainly inclined toward the central powers, and there had long existed a possibility that she would accede to the Triple Alliance. Appended to the treaties of 1882 had been supplementary declarations by all three parties to the alliance that the provisions of the treaties were not directed against England.[3] These declarations were dropped from succeeding treaties. But in the final protocol of 1891 there was registered an express wish for the accession of England to the stipulations of the treaty regarding North Africa, since (as it stated) her accession was already assured to those regarding the Near East.[4] Also in Article X of that treaty it is provided that, in case Italy should undertake an occupation of territory or other action in North Africa with German support, the two powers would seek to place themselves likewise in agreement with England.

Thus toward Great Britain the friendly attitude of the Triple Alliance, and therefore of Germany, its major member, had been implicit in the formal instruments of alliance. Great Britain was, of course, ignorant of the precise terms of the treaties; and, even if informed, she could hardly have placed much reliance upon their guarded and self-interested declarations.

[3] Pribram, *The Secret Treaties of Austria-Hungary, 1879–1914,* I, 69.

[4] *Ibid.,* I, 161.

Nevertheless, throughout the eighties and into the nineties the indulgence of the Triple Alliance for the great neutral was by way of becoming a tradition in European diplomacy.

That tradition had become somewhat dimmed, however, during the three or four years preceding the Fashoda incident. For at least that long Anglo-German relations had been under strain of colonial matters in general and Africa in particular. After the African partition treaty of 1890 between the two powers it was to have been expected that both sides would remit somewhat their earlier rivalries. Salisbury seemed satisfied with his bargain, as was also the German Emperor.[5] Caprivi was a moderate man, not given to peremptory dealings with foreign powers. So, too, was the aged Hohenlohe. Matters might have rested indefinitely.

But about 1894 the young emperor became almost his own foreign minister, and the restless ambitions of *Weltpolitik* began to inspire German policy. The Kaiser had already lost some of the confidence of the British government[6] when in 1896 he almost wantonly destroyed what was left of it by launching his indiscreet telegram of congratulation to Kruger after the Jameson raid. In England it was regarded as a gratuitous provocation, and remained long unforgotten. In Germany it confirmed public opinion in an un-

[5] *The Kaiser's Memoirs, 1888–1918*, pp. 56–57.

[6] *Grosse Politik*, XVII, No. 5019, p. 84, memorandum by Holstein June 14, 1901; Eckardstein, *Ten Years at the Court of St. James*, pp. 57–59.

wholesome belief that the raid was not only a breach of law but somehow also an attack upon German interests.[7]

Thereafter other matters, some of them trivial, worked incessant irritation. The press in both countries exploited every grievance, great or small. The Emperor was much annoyed by the British *Zeitungs Expektorationen*,[8] but he failed, on his own part, to moderate the German newspapers. In 1896 during a strike in Hamburg, England was charged with fomenting socialist disturbances. The affair was actually made the subject of a diplomatic correspondence, the Kaiser almost demanding of Salisbury an official denial, and Salisbury hotly retorting that "the imputation is so devoid of foundation that an official denial would be received [in England] with ridicule."[9] In 1897 (May 30) the British government denounced the Anglo-German trade treaty of 1865, and the German government felt aggrieved. When the *Norddeutsche Allgemeine Zeitung* suggested that the repudiation of the treaty was perhaps only a manifestation of England's close economic union with her colonies, and was directed rather against the United States than against Germany, the Emperor burst out in one of his intem-

[7] *G.P.*, XIII, No. 3403, p. 15, memorandum by Marschall, April 17, 1897.

[8] *Ibid.*, XIII, No. 3396, p. 4, Kaiser to Hohenlohe, October 25, 1896; *British Documents*, I, No. 63, p. 43, Lascelles to Salisbury, February 1, 1898.

[9] *G.P.*, XIII, No. 3400, p. 9, Salisbury to Lascelles, November 30, 1896.

perate marginals, "Unsinn! gegen Deutschland."[10] He
told the imperial chancellor that it was like the beginning of a war to the knife upon German trade; and he
did not fail to draw the moral of the necessity for a
strong navy. German naval weakness was yet another sore point. A navy needed coaling-stations, and
none was to be had except by Great Britain's consent
—an undignified position at best for Germany.[11]

In South Africa, meanwhile, Germany watched
Great Britain with a mixture of envy and indignation;
envy of Britain's opportunities for aggrandizement,
indignation (no doubt sincere) on behalf of the Boer
republic. There were suspicions that England—or
rather Mr. Rhodes abetted by Mr. Chamberlain—had
designs not consistent with existing treaties or with
German interests.[12] But how could Germany intervene without a fleet? And could she count with any
confidence upon the effectual assistance of other powers? Would it not be more prudent to entice England
into an understanding? to permit her, say, to seize
Delagoa Bay, and then make that the starting-point
for a partition of all Portugal's possessions?[13] The
prospect of a deal of that sort would be lost if there
should be a breach with England over the Transvaal.
And besides, if she were not too abruptly crossed, Eng-

[10] *Ibid.,* XIII, No. 3413, p. 33, Monts to Hohenlohe, July 31,
1897.

[11] *The Kaiser's Memoirs,* pp. 69–70.

[12] *G.P.,* XIII, No. 3403, p. 13, memorandum by Marschall,
April 17, 1897.

[13] *Ibid.,* XIII, No. 3404, pp. 17–21, Hatzfeldt to Hohenlohe,
April 22, 1897.

land might even do Germany some services in Asia as
well as in Africa.

With these considerations in mind, instructions
were sent in May, 1897, to Hatzfeldt to sound Salisbury on a general Anglo-German understanding.[14]
This was the first of two such diplomatic ventures in
the eighteen months preceding the Fashoda crisis; the
one on Germany's initiative, the other on Great Britain's.

Hatzfeldt moved very discreetly. He took the precaution, an old and not very subtle trick in diplomacy,
of assuring Salisbury that for months he had not
heard from Berlin anything at all touching South Africa. But he blandly reminded Salisbury that the English had not done so badly in Africa in the days of
good feeling with Germany, when they had got Zanzibar by the cession of a useless rock in the sea. Salisbury met Hatzfeldt's insinuations by emphatically
disclaiming any designs upon the Portuguese colonies,
but Hatzfeldt got the impression that he was not disin-
clined toward an Anglo-German understanding, providing the conditions were not too high.[15]

The German ambassador continued under orders
from home to pursue these veiled negotiations through
the summer and autumn of 1897. The discussions
touched discursively upon China, where Salisbury
thought there was no hurry as the Russian railway

[14] *Ibid.*, XIII, No. 3405, p. 21, Hohenlohe to Hatzfeldt, May
2, 1897.

[15] *Ibid.*, XIII, No. 3407, pp. 25–26, Hatzfeldt to Hohenlohe,
May 12, 1897.

was still far from completion; also upon the United States-Hawaiian treaty of annexation and the Samoan condominium. Hatzfeldt proposed joint representations in Washington, and perhaps a partition of Samoa between England and Germany.[16]

But Salisbury's inertia was proof against these incitements. He conveniently discovered that a half-forgotten Anglo-French treaty of 1843 stood in the way of an Anglo-German agreement over Hawaii;[17] and he seemed, besides, very reluctant to undertake a *démarche* at Washington. As for Samoa, Salisbury made excuse that Australia would never consent to its alienation—"You are asking me to poke my head into a wasp's nest."[18]

Matters did not progress. Salisbury did not, indeed, at any time give a point-blank refusal to Hatzfeldt's various proposals, but he pleaded the difficulties of his government's position. His own foreign policies were not entirely in favor, he said, and the jingoes were hot against him.[19] By December the negotiations had dragged out almost to extinction. In admitting that nothing useful had been accomplished Lord Salisbury besought Hatzfeldt, however, not to lose pa-

[16] *Ibid.,* XIII, No. 3410, pp. 29–30, Hatzfeldt to Hohenlohe, July 22, 1897.

[17] *Ibid.,* XIII, No. 3416, p. 36, Hatzfeldt to Hohenlohe, August 11, 1897.

[18] *Ibid.,* XIII, No. 3418, p. 40, Hatzfeldt to Hohenlohe, September 27, 1897; No. 3422, p. 45, Hatzfeldt to Foreign Office, December 10, 1897.

[19] *Ibid.,* XIII, No. 3420, p. 44, Hatzfeldt to Foreign Office, November 20, 1897.

tience; and he contended in palliation of his conduct that should the British cabinet propose prematurely a *rapprochement* with Germany they would achieve the very opposite of their intentions.[20]

But with the close of the year events in the Far East must have made the British government again aware of the embarrassing consequences of isolation. On November 14 a German squadron had suddenly occupied Kiao-chau; and the German government was very slow in vouchsafing an official explanation or in declaring their intentions. Then before the British government had recovered from their displeasure, Russia took them unawares from the other flank. On January 12 Muravieff announced to the British ambassador at St. Petersburg that the Russian fleet would winter in Port Arthur as a temporary measure; and on the same day the Russian ambassador in London told Lord Salisbury that the British ships in Port Arthur "had produced a bad impression in Russia."[21] Thus Great Britain was being elbowed from both sides and as if by conspiracy. Indeed, shortly afterward (February 7) the British government received evidence that there was some sort of collusive agreement between Germany and Russia; for the German Emperor told Sir Frank Lascelles that the Emperor of Russia had given his consent to the German proposals for action in China.[22]

[20] *Ibid.*, XIII, No. 3423, p. 46, Hatzfeldt to Hohenlohe, December 18, 1897.

[21] *British Documents,* I, 2, memorandum by J. A. C. Tilley.

[22] *Ibid.*, I, No. 4, p. 4, Lascelles to Salisbury, February 2, 1898.

As toward Germany, Lord Salisbury did not set forth any ground of legal complaint; and although he found fault with the abrupt methods employed at Kiao-chau yet he admitted to the German ambassador that he "thought it probable that no great injury had been inflicted upon England."[23] Against Russia, however, he seemed to have a case. But instead of pressing it too closely, he attempted first to come to an accommodation with Russia.

Accordingly, Sir N. O'Conor approached both Witte and Muravieff with intimations that it might yet be possible for England and Russia to work together in China. These overtures met with unexpected favor. Muravieff declared himself ready to consider any proposal which would bring about an entente.[24] Witte roundly called the German action at Kiao-chau an act of brigandage, and wanted to know how far England would go with Russia to hold Germany in check in the Far East.[25] Thus encouraged, Salisbury proceeded to sketch a partition of spheres of influence with a scheme of allotments not only in China but in the Turkish Empire as well.[26] The Russian Emperor himself seemed well disposed, and on February 22 notified his approval of the negotiations.[27]

Nevertheless, the affair did not prosper, and it is

[23] *Ibid.*, I, No. 3, p. 4, Salisbury to Lascelles, January 12, 1898.

[24] *Ibid.*, I, No. 6, p. 6, O'Conor to Salisbury, January 20, 1898.

[25] *Ibid.*, I, No. 8, p. 7, O'Conor to Salisbury, January 23, 1898.

[26] *Ibid.*, I, No. 9, p. 8, Salisbury to O'Conor, January 25, 1898.

[27] *Ibid.*, I, No. 20, p. 15, O'Conor to Salisbury, February 22, 1898.

probable that from the first the project of an entente was hopeless. For the Russians already had an informal understanding with Germany regarding Port Arthur which relieved them of the necessity of making terms with England. On December 14, 1897, Muravieff had sent confidential news to Berlin of the Russian intention to seize Port Arthur, and had at the same time expressed a belief that Germany and Russia could "aller la main dans la main" in the Far East. To which communication *(bon message)* Bülow replied on December 17, most cordially approving the "energetic as well as prudent measure" about to be taken by Russia.[28] By the middle of March, therefore, it began to be apparent to the British government that the Russians were not sincere, and it was suspected that the Emperor's assent to the negotiations had been merely an *acquit de conscience* toward his English relatives.[29] The Russian government raised difficulties over British financial engagements to the Chinese government, and they made it quite clear that with or without British consent they would stick to Port Arthur. But Port Arthur was the main issue in hand. And when on March 23 and 24 each side restated its contentions on that point without modification,[30] no arrangement seemed possible and the negotiations were dropped.

[28] *G.P.*, XIV, No. 3733, p. 121, Muravieff to Osten-Sacken, December 14, 1897; No. 3734, p. 122, Bülow to Osten-Sacken, December 17, 1897.

[29] *British Documents*, I, No. 24, p. 17, memorandum by Bertie, March 14, 1898.

[30] *Ibid.*, I, No. 37, p. 24, O'Conor to Salisbury, March 23; No. 38, p. 24, Salisbury to O'Conor, March 24.

It is notable that it was also on March 24 that Hatzfeldt reported from London to the German government that Alfred Rothschild had arranged a meeting for him with Chamberlain and Balfour. Thus it was immediately on the failure of the Anglo-Russian negotiations that a new series of conversations was inaugurated between Hatzfeldt and members of the British cabinet. This time, however, the overtures came from the side of England, with Hatzfeldt in the posture of reserve and reluctance. The German ambassador was invited to a breakfast to meet some of the ministers. It was the beginning, as he had divined it would be, of an attempt to sound him on a *rapprochement* with Germany.[31] Subsequently, he met in long interviews Balfour, Chamberlain, and, some weeks later, Salisbury. This time the discussions did not revolve vaguely about possible and fragmentary agreements over Samoa, China, or Delagoa Bay, but dealt directly with a close defensive alliance between Germany and Great Britain.

The three British ministers who in turn conducted the negotiations seemed not to be precisely of the same mind, although perhaps the differences lay rather in temperament than in opinion. Balfour, who was in charge of the Foreign Office during Salisbury's sick-leave, proceeded with some caution. He expressed friendliness for Germany, observed that the two powers had no opposing interests, and hinted at the advantages of a *rapprochement*. But as in the beginning he

[31] *G.P.,* XIV, No. 3779, p. 193, Hatzfeldt to Foreign Office, March 24, 1898.

had confined himself to recommending better relations between the two countries, without expressly formulating proposals, so later on when Hatzfeldt had revealed his reluctance, Balfour talked only of a gradual reconciliation beginning in small things, and of putting off to the future a fuller and more intimate political union.[32]

Chamberlain, on the other hand, charged straight at the issue. England, he said, could no longer maintain her traditional policy of isolation. The situation compelled the British government to face at last the necessity of taking grave resolutions; they wished to abandon isolation for an understanding with Germany—which would amount to Great Britain's accession to the Triple Alliance.[33] German and British interests were the same particularly in China, where Russia was constantly pressing forward and would, he reminded Hatzfeldt, eventually threaten German as well as British trade interests.[34] When Hatzfeldt seemed to draw back from the implications of these aggressive proposals, Chamberlain hedged only very slightly by assuring the German ambassador that Great Britain had no thought of contesting the advantages which Russia had already won in China. But he argued that Russian policy would not content itself with relatively small results, and that then Germany

[32] *Ibid.,* XIV, No. 3781, p. 195, Hatzfeldt to Foreign Office, March 25, 1898; Nos. 3786–88, pp. 207–12.

[33] *Ibid.,* XIV, No. 3782, p. 197, Hatzfeldt to Foreign Office, March 29, 1898.

[34] *Ibid.,* XIV, No. 3784, p. 203, Hatzfeldt to Foreign Office, April 1, 1898.

would be involved in preventing the hinterland of Kiao-chau from falling into Russian hands. His object, he said, was to co-operate with the Triple Alliance in barring the Russian advance.[35] Chamberlain must have been nourishing the rash assumption that he was carrying Hatzfeldt with him, for on May 13, in a speech at Birmingham, he openly avowed Britain's need of an alliance and expressly urged an alliance with Germany.[36]

Chamberlain struck Hatzfeldt as a naïf beginner in foreign politics, who consulted principally his own vanity, and who was striving for a personal triumph as the initiator of an alliance with the central powers.[37] Nevertheless, even Lord Salisbury was compelled to take account of him. The German Emperor had remarked contemptuously, "Chamberlain hat Salisbury völlig in der Tasche!"[38] It was an exaggeration, for Salisbury still had the last word in England's foreign policy.[39] Yet it was a question how far the prime minister might not be agreed with the colonial secretary. It was possible that Chamberlain had persuaded his chief, who was now back in England, that the constituency was dissatisfied with the conduct of foreign af-

[35] *Ibid.*, XIV, No. 3793, p. 223, Hatzfeldt to Hohenlohe, April 26, 1898.

[36] *Ibid.*, XIV, No. 3795, p. 229, Hatzfeldt to Foreign Office, May 14, 1898.

[37] *Ibid.*, XIV, No. 3789, p. 215, Hatzfeldt to Hohenlohe, April 7, 1898.

[38] *Ibid.*, XIV, No. 3798, p. 239, marginal.

[39] *Ibid.*, XIV, No. 3801, p. 245, Hatzfeldt to Hohenlohe, June 3, 1898.

fairs and that something ought to be done to strength-
en the government's position.

That did not mean, however, that Salisbury was
ready to follow Chamberlain's adventurous lead to its
extreme consequences. Salisbury held the view, certainly, that the public opinion of Germany and England ought to be brought to a reconciliation, and that
both governments should lead the way by mutual concessions *(nehmen und geben)*.[40] But Salisbury mistrusted on principle all treaties of alliance, which,
he thought, were not to be relied upon in a pinch.
And especially he seemed to disapprove Chamberlain's
scheme for an alliance directed against Russia. At
most he aimed at mutual protection and peace.[41] Moreover, Salisbury was apprehensive lest Germany should
make immoderate demands as the price of an alliance.
And, indeed, the Germans were at that moment pon-
dering just how to make the longest shot without
breaking the bow: one of the Philippine Islands was
thought of in an exchange of compensations. But Salisbury wouldn't hear of it, for he was then sedulously
cultivating good relations with the United States.[42]

Salisbury need not, however, have given himself
any concern, for Bülow had no intention of accommo-
dating Chamberlain, or Salisbury either, with a German alliance. In his dispatches to Hatzfeldt he set

[40] *Ibid.*, XIV, Nos. 3797–98, pp. 233–38, Hatzfeldt to Foreign
Office and to Hohenlohe, May 15 and 20, 1898.

[41] *Ibid.*, XIV, No. 3800, p. 241, Hatzfeldt to Foreign Office,
June 2, 1898.

[42] *Ibid.*, XIV, No. 3801, p. 242, Hatzfeldt to Hohenlohe, June
3, 1898.

forth his views: The weak point in the British proposals was that any arrangement which could be made would bind only the British government of the day. It would be quite in keeping with the character of British democracy simply to vote down and turn out the government which had made the pledges, and then to revert to the old attitude of selfish detachment. Germany had no security against England's sudden disavowal of inconvenient engagements.[43]

Chamberlain did not, of course, admit the force of an argument based on the presumption of British perfidy. But in any case he did not, he said, advocate a mere secret treaty between governments. His idea was that the agreement should be presented openly to Parliament for ratification.[44] Even so, in Bülow's view, an alliance with Great Britain would be a blunder. Germany was not threatened by Russia at any point either in or out of Europe. Why then needlessly bind herself to Russia's chief enemy?[45] An alliance with England would in any case have its point turned against Russia, just as an alliance with Russia would be of necessity aimed at England. Therefore, the Emperor was justified in refusing to be bound to either side.[46]

[43] *Ibid.,* XIV, No. 3783, p. 200, Bülow to Hatzfeldt, March 30, 1898.

[44] *Ibid.,* XIV, No. 3784, p. 202, Hatzfeldt to Foreign Office, April 1, 1898.

[45] *Ibid.,* XIV, No. 3785, p. 205, Bülow to Hatzfeldt, April 3, 1898.

[46] *Ibid.,* XIV, No. 3802, p. 249, Bülow to Kaiser, June 5, 1898; B. E. Schmitt, "Triple Alliance and Triple Entente," *American Historical Review,* XXIX (April, 1927), 454.

While Salisbury was dubiously drawing down the lip at Chamberlain's novelties, and Bülow on his side was advising his sovereign to beware of binding friendships, there seemed little hope of an Anglo-German alliance. And in any case public opinion in both countries would hardly have permitted its standing prejudices to be trifled with. These two very recent failures to come to a general agreement left Anglo-German relations hanging doubtful in the autumn of 1898. Certainly it could not be said that they had been materially improved; and they may even have been somewhat injured by the discovery of so much reluctance on both sides.

But, failing a general alliance, it was still possible and no doubt expedient for Great Britain and Germany to arrive at particular agreements. And at this very moment an opportunity presented itself, and that, too, in Africa.

Portugal was chronically in financial straits; and in June (1898) M. de Soveral had been sent from Lisbon to London in search of a loan. No difficulty was to be anticipated; for while Portugal never had funds in hand, yet she had vast territories in Africa which could stand as excellent security to creditors. But when the rumor got about that these African possessions were to be put in pledge against a British loan, both Germany and France took exception to the transaction. The two continental powers might have combined to frustrate Great Britain's imperialistic finance, and there was a tentative move in that direction. But the German government quickly made up its mind to treat on its own account instead directly and privately with Great Britain on the basis of a division of spoils.

Representations were at once made to Lord Salisbury that any alienation of Portugal's colonial rights should be preceded by an understanding between Germany and England as the most interested neighboring African powers. And Lord Salisbury complied so far as to promise that he would keep Hatzfeldt informed of anything which might touch Germany's legitimate interests.[47] He tried, however, to stave off the inconvenience of a partnership with Germany in any project of partition by insisting that the Portuguese loan, so long as it was free of political implications, was a matter which properly concerned only England and Portugal; that when and if Portugal should dispose of her African colonies, it would then be time enough to consider territorial questions.[48] But the Germans were not to be put off. In his instructions to Hatzfeldt, Bülow pointed out that Germany had refrained from making difficulties in Egypt, but that she could not go on rendering services for nothing *(Frondienst)*; there must be adequate reciprocity. This was suspiciously like a game of blackmail. And farther along in the same dispatch there was another veiled threat: to form a coalition of continental powers against Eng-

[47] *G.P.,* XIV, No. 3807, p. 261, Hatzfeldt to Foreign Office, June 14, 1898; *British Documents,* I, No. 66, p. 48, Salisbury to Gough, June 14, 1898.

[48] *Ibid.,* XIV, No. 3817, p. 270, Hatzfeldt to Foreign Office, June 21, 1898; *British Documents,* I, No. 67, p. 49, Salisbury to Gough, June 21, 1898.

land, a course which Germany would rather avoid, and
Salisbury should not drive her into it by inconsider-
ate treatment.[49]

Thus pressed, Salisbury frankly asked Germany's
price, and with only a very little higgling offered to
pay it. The final negotiations were left to Balfour;
and when at first he showed a tendency to defer to his
colleague, the hard-trafficking Chamberlain, and to
beat down the German demands, it looked as if the
transaction might after all fall through.[50] But Balfour wanted a settlement, and at the end of August
(only a few days before Kitchener arrived at Fashoda), a convention was framed which conceded Germany's full demands. Both governments were to have
the right to participate in loans to Portugal. Great
Britain was to be secured by the revenues of Mozam-
bique south of the Zambezi, and of Angola north of
Egito. Germany was to be secured by the revenues of
the remainder of the two provinces, and by those of
Portuguese Timor. By secret articles it was also
agreed that neither Great Britain nor Germany would
advance territorial or political claims in those parts of
the Portuguese colonies whose revenues had been assigned to the other.[51]

Some months later (July, 1899) the German min-

[49] *Ibid.,* XIV, No. 3818, pp. 273–74, Bülow to Hatzfeldt, June
22, 1898. Cf. also *British Documents,* I, No. 78, p. 59, Salisbury to
Gough, July 20, 1898.

[50] *G.P.,* XIV, Nos. 3851–52, pp. 318–20, Hatzfeldt to Foreign
Office, August 17–18, 1898; *British Documents,* I, No. 87, p. 69,
Lascelles to Balfour, August 22, 1898.

[51] *G.P.,* XIV, No. 3872, pp. 347 ff., text of convention.

ister at Lisbon admitted unreservedly to his British colleague that he had understood his instructions to mean that one of the objects of the Anglo-German agreement was to induce Portugal to contract a loan in order that when the proceeds had been wasted Germany and England might enter upon a control of the Portuguese customs.[52]

But by the convention Germany gained nothing, either then or thereafter. It was an agreement based on a contingency which never arose. And Great Britain, who had been beguiled too easily, soon repented her jobbery, and did not even wait to see what the future might bring forth. For late in the following year the ancient Anglo-Portuguese treaty was renewed by the Treaty of Windsor, which guaranteed to Portugal the very territories in which England and Germany had been speculating.[53] Therefore, the convention never came into operation. Fifteen years afterward the project of a partition of the Portuguese colonies was to be revived between Great Britain and Germany, only to be again brought to naught by the intervention of the great war.[54]

Nevertheless, Great Britain derived an indirect advantage, at least, from her momentary complaisance toward Germany in Africa. For by a sort of hypothecation Germany's present neutrality in African affairs had been purchased against the crisis which arose

[52] *British Documents,* I, No. 112, p. 86, MacDonell to Salisbury, July 22, 1899.

[53] *Ibid.,* I, No. 118, pp. 98–99, October 14, 1899, text.

[54] *Cambridge History of British Foreign Policy,* III, 477.

in the very month of the exchange of ratifications.
During the negotiations of the summer of 1898 the
German Foreign Office had called special attention to
the value of the arrangement as precluding the possibility of an Anglo-French war over South Africa. It
was also pointed out that any evidence that Germany
stood by England even on a single question could not
but be favorable to England's general position.[55] And
afterward Bülow asserted (May 6, 1899) that French
diffidence in the Fashoda affair would have been un-
thinkable if England had not had a feeling of confidence toward Germany.[56] There was truth in the contention, and that was Salisbury's reward for what to
the jingoes seemed at the moment but another and
characteristic weakness. His soft answer had postponed Germany's wrath to a more convenient season.
Germany was for the moment placated, and England's
isolation was once more splendid.

Unlike Great Britain, France was traditionally on
bad terms with Germany. But it happened that, for
reasons already suggested, France, like Great Britain,
had recently been cultivating better relations with her
eastern neighbor.

The new master of Germany in discarding some of
the Bismarckian traditions had also assumed an attitude of rather theatrical generosity toward France.

[55] *G.P.*, XIV, No. 3856, p. 323, Richthofen to Hatzfeldt, August 20, 1898.

[56] *Ibid.*, XIV, No. 4021, p. 549, Bülow to Hatzfeldt, May 6,
1899.

His public acts and utterances, while not always consistent with a policy of peace, seemed often aimed at beguiling France from her settled hostility. He flattered the French delegates to the Labor Convention in Berlin (1890) ; he expressed sympathy on the death of Marshal MacMahon in 1893; he took occasion to eulogize French valor on the anniversaries of the war of 1870.[57] When a certain French naval attaché in Berlin came under a cloud for duelling (January, 1897), the Emperor passed lightly over the offense and sententiously quoted his grandfather in defense of a resort to the sword as the *ultima ratio* in matters of honor.[58] He telegraphed sympathy for the victims of a fatal fire in a fashionable charity bazaar in May, 1897.[59] He even inquired formally after the health of General Gallifet, who had been ill.[60] And when, in July, 1897, a bomb was thrown at the French President's carriage while driving in the Bois, the Emperor sent his felicitations that God had preserved his life to France.[61] To these civilities the French government did not fail to make proper returns; and Münster was

[57] Tardieu, *France and the Alliances,* p. 151.

[58] *G.P.,* XIII, Nos. 3453–55, pp. 93–95, Kaiser, Münster, and Hohenlohe, January 22–26, 1897.

[59] *Ibid.,* XIII, No. 3458, p. 97, Münster to Hohenlohe, May 7, 1897.

[60] *Ibid.,* XIII, No. 3456, p. 95, Münster to Hohenlohe, February 8, 1897.

[61] *Ibid.,* XIII, No. 3462, p. 101, Kaiser to President Faure, June 13, 1897.

pressed to accept the grand cross of the Legion of Honor.[62]

That the Emperor's blandishments were not entirely successful is evidenced by the tone of a part of the French press as reported by Münster. The past could not be effaced by these easy courtesies from "le petit fils de nos vainqueurs"; there were too many persistent suspicions and ancient resentments. Nevertheless, there were no doubt many Frenchmen who sincerely regretted the old and implacable bitterness. More than that, there had grown up in some circles a spirit of obsequious *Germanolatrie*. By 1895 a faction of the French intellectuals were giving fulsome allegiance to the superiority of German culture; were congratulating themselves that the miseries of 1870 were finding compensation in the intellectual gifts proffered by the victors. The ideal of patriotism was sneered at as "cette vieille idole anthropophage." And even politicians averred that in Africa the two nations had the same interests, and that a colonial alliance could well be of advantage to both parties.[63] The spirit of *revanche* itself seemed to be waning. Münster reported (December, 1897) that, while the older generation perhaps still held fast to ideas of revenge, the younger almost entirely regarded the Frankfort Peace as a historical fact. Even the army, he said, did not want

[62] *Ibid.,* XIII, No. 3470, p. 109, Münster to Hohenlohe, December 31, 1897.

[63] Maurras, *Quand les Français ne s'aimaient pas,* pp. 2–6.

war with Germany; and the hope of recovering Alsace-Lorraine without assistance was steadily dwindling.[64]

The French government itself also had been ready to accept tenders of good will from Germany, and for reasons of its own was glad of the Emperor's policy of relaxation and advances. M. Hanotaux, who was foreign minister from 1894 to the early summer of 1898, was an ardent expansionist, and was therefore hostile to the British empire rather than to Germany. And if for no other reason, then at least for the sake of colonial expansion, it was necessary to keep on good terms with Germany. Accordingly, when the powers were invited to participate in celebrating the opening of the Kiel Canal, France accepted with the rest. There were protests in the Chambre, and the memories of 1871 were invoked; but Hanotaux was able to defend his action on the rather hollow plea that it was impossible to meet courtesy with discourtesy.[65] Also the French government joined the German and the Russian in the Far East in nullifying the terms of the treaty of Shimonoseki. In his *Memoirs* the Kaiser remarks that

making common cause with the Franco-Russian group offered the possibility of achieving gradually a more trusting and less strained relationship in Europe and of living side by side with our two neighbours there in more friendliness as a result of the common policy adopted in the Far East.[66]

[64] *G.P.*, XIII, No. 3432, p. 69, Münster to Hohenlohe, April 7, 1897; No. 3469, p. 108.

[65] Schefer, *D'une guerre à l'autre,* p. 196.

[66] *The Kaiser's Memoirs,* p. 82.

And certainly to have co-operated at all with Germany necessitated at least an exchange of views, and implied a certain accord if nothing more. From 1896 onward there had been rumors afloat that secret overtures were being made by Berlin for common Franco-German action in Africa.[67] Perhaps the Kaiser's telegram to Kruger was sent in expectation of French support. At any rate, Marschall, the German foreign secretary, invited the French ambassador in Berlin to examine with him how far France would join in limiting the "insatiable appetite" of England,[68] and the German papers reproached France with unwillingness to co-operate against Great Britain in the Transvaal.

There is, however, no evidence that thus far Hanotaux had undertaken serious negotiations in Berlin touching African matters. But France was now (1896) proposing to engage in a deliberate contest with Great Britain in that continent. These were the years in which Hanotaux was launching Liotard and Marchand upon their enterprises on the Upper Ubangi. He was deliberately embarking in a race for territory upon the principle of "à chacun selon ses oeuvres," and was pressing westward in defiance of Grey's "Monroe Doctrine" for the Nile Valley. Hanotaux has repudiated the conception of his policy as one systematically hostile to Great Britain.[69] He has pointed out that he was even then carrying on negotia-

---

[67] Darcy, *France et Angleterre,* pp. 103 ff.

[68] Gooch, *History of Modern Europe,* p. 218.

[69] Hanotaux, *Fachoda,* p. 105.

tions with Great Britain for the delimitation of spheres in West Africa—negotiations which after long delays were to result in the Anglo-French Agreement of June 14, 1898. But the Marchand mission was not recalled, and it was in itself admittedly an act of covert hostility against Great Britain. It was certainly "une politique d'action résolument opposée aux projets de l'Angleterre."[70] It was imperative, therefore, that French diplomacy should make ready against the apparently inevitable shock, and Hanotaux himself felt that time was pressing.[71]

In the early months of 1897 the French government found an opportunity to come to an agreement with Germany in West Africa, and negotiations were undertaken. Münster thought Hanotaux more ready to settle than was the minister of colonies; which is what might be expected from Hanotaux' preoccupation with German relations.[72] In April Hohenlohe, the German chancellor, came to Paris; and Hanotaux' interview with him considerably advanced the negotiations.[73] In July a treaty was signed which disposed of the hinterland of Togo and Dahomey. The French minister was very well pleased, and expressed a belief that Franco-German relations would now improve.[74]

[70] *Ibid.*, p. 104.

[71] *Ibid.*, p. 112.

[72] *G.P.*, XIII, No. 3457, p. 96, Münster to Hohenlohe, April 7, 1897.

[73] Hanotaux, *op. cit.*, p. 114.

[74] *G.P.*, XIII, No. 3467, p. 105, Münster to Hohenlohe, July 24, 1897.

Something at least had been done by diplomacy, while in Africa itself Liotard was already at Deim Zubeir in the Bahr-el-Ghazelle.[75]

It was a modest success, but the British government may nevertheless have been impressed, for Hanotaux found them more conciliatory in the summer and autumn of 1897. The Niger negotiations were therefore resumed, and throughout the winter Hanotaux was employed in framing an agreement with Great Britain. But no further advance had been made in the direction of a more general understanding with Germany when in June the Méline cabinet fell and Hanotaux was out of office, his task barely begun.

Before the new cabinet was formed, however, and while Hanotaux was still in charge at the Quay d'Orsay, the question of the Portuguese colonies and the English loan fell under the notice of both Paris and Berlin. It was a matter in which France might have intervened with as much propriety as Germany. Bülow, in writing to Münster, hinted pointedly that both powers had the same interest in preventing a change in Portugal's *status quo*. There was apparently no obstacle, therefore, to a mutual understanding, and perhaps to joint representations in Lisbon and London. To Hanotaux it may even have occurred that here at last was offered providentially in Africa ground for common action with Germany against Great Britain. Whether, therefore, Berlin first broached the matter or Paris does not seem to be of much consequence; it is at least certain that the Portuguese colonies became

[75] For text of convention, Hanotaux, *op. cit.,* Annexe, p. 328.

the subject of certain diplomatic passages between the two. On the one hand, the French ambassador in Berlin questioned Bülow about the "suspicious negotiations" going on in London and, on the other, Bülow authorized Münster to approach Hanotaux upon the same topic.[76]

Hanotaux, when interviewed and presented with a memorandum by the German ambassador (June 19), seemed to be decidedly of opinion that an energetic remonstrance must be made in Lisbon against any scheme for alienating the Portuguese colonies; and Münster's impression was that the French minister was personally inclined to make common cause with Germany in this as in any other questions which might touch the interests of both powers.[77] A few days later (June 22) the French envoy in Lisbon denounced the special negotiations with England as unnecessary and dangerous,[78] and on the same day the German minister told the King of Portugal that "the Emperor would not continue on amicable terms with Portugal" if due regard were not paid to "the legitimate interests of Germany in her African colonies."[79]

Hanotaux' attitude should have been entirely satisfactory to the German government if they really sought French co-operation. But a minister ad in-

[76] *G.P.*, XIV, No. 3813, p. 267, Bülow to Münster, June 18, 1898.

[77] *Ibid.*, XIV, No. 3814, p. 268, Münster to Foreign Office, June 19, 1898.

[78] *Ibid.*, XIV, No. 3818, p. 272, Bülow to Hatzfeldt, June 22, 1898.

[79] *British Documents*, I, No. 68, p. 50, Salisbury to Mac-Donell, June 22, 1898.

terim could not bind the incoming French government; and it fell to Delcassé, the new foreign minister, to decide upon a policy and to dispose finally of the memorandum which Münster had addressed to his predecessor.

M. Delcassé deliberately left the memorandum unanswered. Partisans of an entente with Germany believed it an unpardonable error which compromised all subsequent French policy. On the eve of a conflict with Great Britain, Delcassé had missed, they thought, the unique opportunity of securing for himself an immense tactical advantage; he had been too inexperienced to grasp the true trend of Hanotaux' policy, and too timorous to make bold use of an understanding with Germany. He had not seen and he had not dared. It was argued with almost passionate regret that a Franco-German alignment against Great Britain in the matter of the Portuguese colonies would have carried inestimable consequences in the Fashoda controversy six months later.[80]

It is quite possible, of course, that Delcassé failed to apprehend the requirements of the policy marked out by Hanotaux; that he did not see the part that a German entente might play in colonial affairs and particularly in the approaching crisis. It is also possible that he was reluctant to enter upon a policy of *rapprochement* in which France might be reduced to the rôle of a subordinate and accomplice of Germany. But these explanations of his course are unconvincing, and

[80] Mévil, *De la paix de Francfort à la conférence d'Algésiras,* pp. 13 ff.

especially if it be permitted to judge him then by his subsequent career. It would be hard to convict him, on his own record, of incapacity and timidity. It is much easier to suppose that he had assured himself by the inquiries he made in Lisbon during the summer that the Portuguese colonies were in no danger of alienation, that Germany's professions of anxiety over them lacked sincerity, and that, for the rest, there was as yet no sufficient basis for a general entente with Germany.[81]

But whatever may have been his motives, there is this to be said against the idea that he needlessly rebuffed and estranged Germany: Germany had the least possible intention of co-operating with France in the matter of the Portuguese colonies except as a last shift and in case England should prove unaccommodating. It is quite true that more than once Hatzfeldt made solemn parade to Salisbury of the chance of a Franco-German understanding, and that he gave intimations of the regrettable consequences which might follow upon England's failure to meet Germany's wishes. Germany would then be found, he said, among England's opponents in Lisbon—perhaps in alliance with France. And the opposition there would of itself extend to other matters.[82] But at the very beginning of the business, when the French ambassador in Berlin made first mention of the Portuguese colonies, Bülow

[81] Schefer, *op. cit.*, p. 225.

[82] *G.P.*, XIV, No. 3837, p. 301, Hatzfeldt to Foreign Office, July 20, 1898; No. 3840, p. 305, memorandum by Richthofen, July 23, 1898; *British Documents,* I, No. 81, p. 60, memorandum by Bertie, August 10, 1898.

had replied only evasively, because, as he afterward explained, he hoped to get more from England directly than by associating Germany with France.[83] And a few days later (June 22) he wrote to Hatzfeldt in London that France was to be left out if England and Germany could come to terms.[84]

It seems, therefore, that the Münster note may have been designed at first to test the ground in France toward a genuine Franco-German accord. It is hard to explain otherwise. But it is also perfectly plain that the other alternative of an understanding with England took first place in the minds of the German government; and that once there was a fair chance of success in London, the idea of co-operating with France was discarded. By the time Delcassé was firmly established in office the opportunity for a German entente —if indeed it ever existed—had quite vanished. Hanotaux himself, therefore, might not have succeeded where Delcassé failed. And for Delcassé to have patched up some sort of reconciliation with Germany at the eleventh hour would have been a truly astonishing feat of improvisation in diplomacy. On one of Münster's reports stating that it was becoming more and more recognized in Paris that a *rapprochement* with Germany would be in the best interests of France, the Kaiser remarked dryly, "Ein bischen spät!"—it

[83] *Ibid.*, XIV, No. 3812, p. 266, Bülow to Hatzfeldt, June 17, 1898.

[84] *Ibid.*, XIV, No. 3818, p. 276, Bülow to Hatzfeldt, June 22, 1898.

should have been done during the Transvaal troubles.[85]

Moreover, it is hard to see what specific benefits France could have expected to reap from a hastily contrived friendship with Germany. Could it be supposed that Germany would have done for her what Russia refused? that Germany, warmed and melted by the new entente, would have backed France against England? Would Bülow, who was ever in dread of burning his fingers with chestnuts for somebody else, have become suddenly so sympathetic and obliging?

It is very difficult, therefore, to accept the view of Delcassé's detractors that Germany's attitude during the Fashoda crisis was based on pique over the slight to Münster's note. The fact was that Germany profoundly distrusted France. It was held in Berlin that, whatever advances any French government might make, no government since Ferry's day had ever been strong enough to carry out a policy of avowed friendship for Germany in spite of French chauvinism.[86] Hanotaux had done very well and had won the toleration of the Imperial government; but Delcassé was still suspect.[87] Bülow judged that in France "the hatred of Germany could not be affected, let alone removed, by ill-feeling against England," that the policy of a generation could not be turned aside by "a misadventure

[85] *Ibid.,* XIV, No. 3911, p. 393, marginal.

[86] *Ibid.,* XIII, No. 3426, p. 58, memorandum by Marschall, January 31, 1897.

[87] *Ibid.,* XIII, No. 3554, p. 241, Münster to Hohenlohe, June 30, 1898.

on a remote track." There may have been, he thought, some disappointment in Paris because "England would not, for the sake of French friendship, sacrifice any of her interests in the Sudan and on the Nile, but France was ready in any case, though with clenched teeth, to pay the price or even a higher one for England's friendship."[88] Perhaps Bülow should have substituted the word tolerance for friendship; for it is improbable that as yet either France or England had given place to any confident hope of cordial relations. But at least he expressed the plain truth that France could not be diverted from her preoccupation in hatred of Germany. It was indisputable that, as De Courcel had once said to Salisbury, France had only one enemy, namely, Germany.[89]

Neither France nor Great Britain, therefore, could have confidently expected the favor of Germany during their dissensions over Fashoda. Hanotaux had failed to win it, although he had been the recipient of many marks of German relenting, and although from the moment he foresaw that the drift of his African policy was carrying him straight toward a collision with Great Britain he had consciously endeavored to conciliate Germany. It may have been his misfortune that he fell from power before he had contrived to complete his design. It seems more probable that he could not have completed it in any case. When he left the Quay d'Orsay in June, nothing tangible had been

[88] Bülow, *Imperial Germany,* p. 106.

[89] *G.P.,* XIV, No. 3877, p. 361, Bülow to Radolin, September 2, 1898.

accomplished; had he remained in office, the Fashoda crisis would almost certainly have overtaken him still unprepared. Delcassé, who took over Foreign Affairs, was more reticent toward Germany. Münster seems from the first to have had a presentiment that the new minister would earn Germany's distrust. He did not like him. Perhaps Delcassé was less sanguine of the possibility of an entente; perhaps he had no belief in the value of the thing itself, and had no premonition of how useful it might be even before the year was out. At any rate, and at least on the surface, his policy was a negation of that of Hanotaux. Germany remained as always the great enemy.

If Great Britain had managed better, she was still far from being either liked or trusted by Germany. Twice in eighteen months she had failed to arrive at a general understanding with Germany upon colonial matters. And the attempts had left behind a train of small resentments. Each government had found the other too hard to deal with. As for the agreement over the Portuguese colonies, it had been extorted from Great Britain under threat of Germany's displeasure and in return for her calculating tolerance. For that Great Britain had been seduced into disloyalty toward an ancient ally. It was an unsavory deal from which Great Britain was fain to extricate herself at the earliest opportunity. And besides, the arrangement with Germany in South Africa had no specific bearing upon the question of the Nile Valley. Germany had even been at pains to make it clear to France and Russia that the agreement with England did not touch the

Egyptian question.[90] It had been a settlement of a particular matter, not a general entente. And lastly, Germany herself must have been only moderately satisfied with the transaction.[91] Its benefits were only contingent, and in the sequel they were illusory. Germany's anticipations in Portugal's crumbling estate had been duly regularized by the agreement. But a mocking fortune delayed the hoped for partition, and it was after all never to come to pass.

As between France and England, therefore, Germany's position in 1898–99 was at least formally neutral. She was not committed either way, and was apparently content to maintain the proprieties as an onlooker. Bülow's idea was that Germany should assume a watchful middle ground, that her attitude should be independent, firm, and equable, with good relations toward both parties, and holding to the pursuit of "nur deutschen Interessen."[92]

But Germany was far from wishing to efface herself. And as affairs stood in Europe, even the most rigid impartiality, the most Olympian disinterestedness from Germany, would not have been without its significance in the Anglo-French dispute. The truth was that German neutrality did not weigh equally on each side; by a sort of paradox German neutrality

[90] *Ibid.*, XIII, No. 3558, p. 251, Huhn of the *Kölnische Zeitung,* December 5, 1898.

[91] *British Documents,* I, No. 112, p. 86, July 22, 1899; No. 121, pp. 98–99, December 20, 1900.

[92] *G.P.,* XIV, No. 3920, p. 399, Bülow to Müller, November 15, 1898.

was not neutral. And the Germans themselves were aware of the fact. Bülow expounded his views on that point in a dispatch to Hatzfeldt earlier in the year (April 24), and before the Fashoda case had arisen. He was trying at the time to represent German good will as quite worth the price then being asked from Great Britain. Germany's neutrality alone, he said, would probably suffice to secure England against a conflict with France and Russia together. He declared that it would interest him to learn whether there was in England a single statesman who seriously believed in the possibility that France could be drawn into a war with England while Germany as neutral stood armed on her flank. It would not be necessary for England to make any sacrifices whatever in order to purchase French complaisance, since that was immediately conditional upon German neutrality; and the latter, Bülow pointed out, was to be had more cheaply. France and Russia were advancing in a policy of expansion, and in no long time they would encroach upon interests which England believed herself bound to defend. At that point France would have to ask herself whether or not she would engage England in war. In Bülow's opinion—and he thought the gentlemen in England should be clear on the matter—the answer France would give to the question would depend far less upon English concessions and promises than upon the menace which under the circumstances might lie in Germany's waiting attitude.[93] The moment fore-

[93] *Ibid.*, XIV, No. 3792, p. 220, Bülow to Hatzfeldt, April 24, 1898.

seen by Bülow had arrived, and Germany remained neutral. But, true to prediction, it was a neutrality which left only Great Britain free. For France it was no more than a further stay of the hand which in twenty-five years had been always ready to strike. A waiting attitude carried no reassurances. France could have had few illusions on that point.

CHAPTER IX

RUSSIA AND THE DISPUTANTS

It might be here objected, however, that so far France has been fallaciously represented as entirely isolated in Europe, as having carried alone her double burden of colonies and *revanche;* that until this moment scarcely any mention has been made of the Russian Alliance. But certainly France had for ally one of the first powers in Europe. And surely she might have taken account of that fact in her present difficulties—as might Germany, too, and England. *Revanche* and reinstatement were but the French rendering of that duplicate antagonism toward Germany which had also a Russian version. As for colonies, China and the Afghan border were the Russian equivalents of West Africa and the Bahr-el-Ghazelle.

And, indeed, it would seem that the Russian Alliance should have been a tower of strength in just such an emergency as this over Fashoda. For six years France had been building her hopes and sustaining her courage upon the Russian Alliance. Ever since the Kronstadt celebrations she had been taking heart from the new-found friendship. The old abject days of timorous circumspection were to be no more. A new era was acclaimed in which affronts need not be tamely swallowed nor encounters ingloriously avoided. And now the moment had come to test these happy assumptions. During the summer of 1898 the French govern-

ment must have known that Marchand was overdue in
the Bahr-el-Ghazelle. And if France knew, then Russia should have known also. But whether or not the
Czar's support was solicited in advance, there could
have been no question that presently the implications
of the Franco-Russian alliance would be plainly exhib-
ited.

In the middle of October three Russian ministers
visited Paris: Muravieff, Witte, and Kuropatkin.
Muravieff came, it was said, to allay the surprise and
annoyance felt in France over the Czar's inconsider-
ateness in summoning (August 12) a conference on
disarmament without having first consulted his ally.
Witte came to see if money was yet to be had in France,
for the Russian treasury was insatiable. And Kuropatkin, minister of war, wished to learn the mood of
the French army.[1] But whatever their ostensible objects may have been, it was inevitable that Fashoda
should fall to be discussed with their French hosts. It
was the moment when Delcassé had already exhausted
the resources of argument against Salisbury, and was
enjoying a short respite while awaiting Marchand's
report. The presence of the Russians in France was of
good omen; the French were no doubt gratified, if for
no other reason then because Europe would be properly impressed with the solidarity of the alliance.

But if Delcassé had been at any time putting his
trust in Russia, he must now have been thoroughly dis-
abused. There proved to be no substance in Russian

[1] *Grosse Politik,* XIV, No. 3892, p. 376, Münster to Hohenlohe, October 17, 1898.

sympathy over Fashoda. The Czar, if he was ever actually consulted, seems in the emergency to have coun-
selled a pacific settlement with England. He may even
have made up his mind in advance not to uphold
France in the quarrel with England. And, indeed, at
that juncture the Imperial Government would have
found grave inconvenience in supporting its ally by
arms; for Russia was low in funds, and its army was
undergoing reorganization. It was perhaps not altogether a coincidence that two months earlier the Czar
had first proposed a European peace conference. At
any rate, while Muravieff was in Paris it was given out
that Russia could not favor a French policy which
might endanger peace.[2] And subsequently it became
known that the help of the Russian fleet had been refused in case of war, and that the French had been
urged to await a better occasion against their adversary.[3]

After Muravieff left Paris he began at once in interviews with representatives of other powers to make
it plain that there would be no war. This was, perhaps, a less pardonable disservice than having privately refused to give aid in case of war, for it was a public
intimation that Russia would stand aside. It has the
look of a rather heartless exposure of Delcassé's hand
while the Frenchman was still valiantly playing his

[2] Barclay, *Thirty Years Anglo-French Reminiscences*, pp.
148 ff.

[3] *G.P.*, XIII, No. 3558, p. 250, Hohn of the *Kölnische Zeitung*, December 5, 1898; *British Documents*, I, No. 215, p. 182,
Monson to Salisbury, October 25, 1898.

game. On his way through Vienna, Muravieff expressed himself warmly over the attitude of Delcassé, in whom he said he had the greatest confidence. The French minister had told him not to concern himself over Fashoda, as it was an affair which touched only France and England and no third power. Muravieff was "most pleasantly surprised," and was now "sure of a peaceful issue."[4] In St. Petersburg he continued to bestow these sanguine assurances. And after Fashoda was evacuated he commended the wisdom and prudence of the French government, which had had the courage to admit and amend the mistakes of former cabinets. He assured Prince Radolin, the German ambassador in St. Petersburg, that Delcassé had acted toward Great Britain without mental reservations; that he had even considered whether he dared not recognize England's provisional position in Egypt as definitive. In Paris Muravieff had found everything quiet: so much talk of war everywhere else was, he said, to be deprecated.[5]

On Radolin's report of these conversations the German Emperor bluntly remarked that Muravieff, "der alte Optimist," did not observe much while he was in Paris. Radolin himself doubted if Muravieff believed his own words, and suggested that he might be only trying to disguise the present weakness of France and to distract attention from Russia's somewhat un-

[4] *G.P.*, XIV, No. 3896, p. 380, Eulenburg to Foreign Office, October 24, 1898; No. 3897, Eulenburg to Hohenlohe.

[5] *Ibid.*, XIV, Nos. 3922, 3924, pp. 401, 404, Radolin to Hohenlohe, December 16 and 21, 1898.

generous conduct. And, indeed, there is hardly the accent of sincerity in Muravieff's utterances, if they have been fairly reported. His praises sound almost like disparagements. There is a shade too much unction in the handsome words he has for Delcassé and his policy, too much protestation of the certainty of peace, as if he were hoping to explain away the scandal of Russia's desertion of an ally. At any rate, it all came to this: that Russia was resolved not to be dragged into a war against England in behalf of France, and was discreetly giving notice of the fact.

This dash to French hopes (if, indeed, France had at any time been counting on Russian support) must have been a bitter experience. But it is doubtful whether in this instance resentment against Russia was altogether justified by circumstances; and, first, because Russia was not interested in Africa. Certain Russians had been more or less implicated in the Fashoda enterprise: a Colonel Artomonoff had accompanied the Sobat expedition of 1898, which attempted a junction from the east with Marchand from the west;[6] and Rennel Rodd found another Russian in Addis Ababa supporting French intrigues at the Abyssinian court.[7] But from all accounts the activities of these men could not be represented as an official participation.

In Egypt the Russians had an interest in evicting Great Britain and Europeanizing the Suez Canal; it

[6] Gleichen, *The Anglo-Egyptian Sudan,* I, 70.

[7] J. Rennel Rodd, *Social and Diplomatic Memories,* Second Series, p. 158.

was a corollary of their general policy in the Levant.
And it will be remembered that in 1896 the Russian
Commissioner of the Debt joined his French colleague
in refusing the Egyptian government the funds asked
for the Dongola campaign. But even in Egypt the
Russians were only mildly concerned. Back in 1891
Ribot and Giers had agreed, during the conversations
which initiated the Franco-Russian alliance, that Rus-
sian interests in Egypt were not considerable, al-
though naturally identical with those of France.[8] And
Ribot later expressed his own opinion that in Egypt
France could expect only moral support from Russia.[9]

Elsewhere in the African continent Russia had
scarcely the shadow of an interest. In 1896 the German ambassador in St. Petersburg had found Prince
Lobanoff, the Foreign Minister, indifferent over the
South African situation, and quite disposed to excuse
England's proceedings in the Transvaal.[10] And in
June, 1898, only three months before the Fashoda
crisis, Muravieff had emphatically dissociated himself
from African affairs. When the German ambassador
had come to him with the news that Great Britain was
about to appropriate the Portuguese colonies as security against a Portuguese loan, Muravieff replied
unconcernedly that Russia had no colonies in Africa,
and could therefore witness such matters quite un-

[8] *Documents Diplomatiques: L'alliance franco-russe,* No. 21,
p. 20, note by Ribot, November 21, 1891.

[9] *Ibid.,* No. 22, p. 24, Ribot to Cambon, December 6, 1891.

[10] *G.P.,* XIV, No. 3877, p. 361, Bülow to Radolin, September
2, 1898.

moved—"Tout ça me laisse absolument froid."[11]
There is yet another instance of Russia's indifference
to Africa. On September 5, on the very eve of Kitchener's and Marchand's encounter, Muravieff told Radolin that Russia wanted nothing in Africa; Russia
had enough to do elsewhere and wanted peace.[12]

The only possible conclusion to be drawn from
these expressions, although they did not bear specific
reference to Fashoda, is that the Russian government
wished Germany to understand that it disengaged itself completely from African concerns. And if the
Germans were so frankly informed of Russia's attitude, it is inconceivable that France had no hint of it.
It would have been inexcusable in France not to have
acquainted herself with the views of her ally.

France may, of course, have preferred at first to
believe that Russia would scarcely decline a quarrel
with her ancient enemy. Both France and Russia had
standing antagonisms against the British empire; and
it seems almost by chance that France had marched
to the decisive encounter in Africa before Russia in
Asia—say in Armenia in 1896 or in China a little
later. There could not, therefore, have been the least
question of Russia's bias in any Anglo-French controversy, nor specifically in this one over Fashoda. A
year before, Prince Radolin had reported from St.
Petersburg (July 4, 1897) that if there was then any

[11] *Ibid.*, XIV, No. 3820, p. 280, Techirischky to Foreign Office, June 23, 1898; No. 3877, p. 361.

[12] *Ibid.*, XIV, No. 3878, p. 362, Radolin to Foreign Office,
September 5, 1898.

certain feature in the physiognomy of Russian policy it was opposition to England.[13] And a little while after (September) Muravieff had charged General Obrutcheff to tell Bülow that he still regarded England as the chief adversary.[14] This burst of frankness may have been ill advised, for Bülow brought the matter confidentially to the knowledge of Lord Salisbury. Nevertheless, Muravieff's hearty declaration against England was probably quite sincere. He was at the time particularly indignant over British policy in the Near East: a specious humanitarianism serving political ends in Armenia and Crete. The young Czar had once told Hohenlohe that the English were responsible for the whole movement in both Armenia and Crete.[15] And on a later occasion in St. Petersburg he had revealed to Bülow also his sentiments toward England. In private talk, and "unter vier Augen," he spoke freely, and he told his German visitors that he wished to live to see England turned out of Egypt.[16] Just recently, moreover (spring, 1898), the British objections to Russian activities in the Far East, and especially to the occupation of Port Arthur, had left the two powers on very bad terms.

Great Britain was perfectly aware of Russia's

[13] *Ibid.*, XIII, No. 3435, p. 72, Radolin to Hohenlohe, July 4, 1897.

[14] *Ibid.*, XIII, No. 3451, p. 89, Bülow to Foreign Office, September 13, 1897.

[15] Hohenlohe, *Memoirs,* II, 483.

[16] *G.P.,* XIII, No. 3444, p. 82, Bülow to Eulenburg, August 20, 1897.

hostility, which for that matter was known to all Europe. Nevertheless, it was notable that at no time either before or after the evacuation of Fashoda did the English seem to give themselves much concern over Russian intervention. In all the English newspaper discussions which had winnowed the Fashoda question to its last grain, it was remarked that Russia was scarcely touched upon. Everywhere the assumption seemed to be that the Russian government would confine itself to a moral support of its ally.[17] Lord Salisbury told Hatzfeldt that he was not in the least perturbed over the prospect; that Russia was out of funds, and that besides England and Russia had no common battleground.[18] Radolin wrote to Hohenlohe from St. Petersburg (December 16) that Sir Charles Scott seemed entirely reassured after interviews with Muravieff and Witte. Sir Charles had learned, he said, that Count Muravieff during his stay in Paris had given the French minister to know without ambiguity that it was necessary to drop Fashoda—"und sich ruhig zu verhalten."[19] From the Englishman's side there is an account of his interview with Witte on November 2, in which the Russian minister seems to have made no specific mention of the current Anglo-French difficulties, a reticence which in itself would be signifi-

[17] Ibid., XIV, No. 3899, p. 382, C.-Rudenhausen to Hohenlohe, October 27, 1898; No. 3909, p. 390, C.-Rudenhausen to Hohenlohe, November 8, 1898.

[18] Ibid., XIV, No. 3925, p. 406, Hatzfeldt to Hohenlohe, December 22, 1898.

[19] Ibid., XIV, No. 3922, p. 402, Radolin to Hohenlohe, December 16, 1898.

cant. But he did say that there was "nothing he had more at heart" than a thorough understanding with Great Britain in China.[20]

England therefore knew, what Germany also knew, and what France perhaps knew before either of them, that Russia was prepared to condone an injury to French interests in Africa. To a good many Frenchmen Russia's conduct may have appeared faithless. Germany would be pleased, no doubt, at this new evidence that the Franco-Russian alliance was without practical efficacy. Prince Hohenlohe had recently been trying to effect a *rapprochement* with Russia; might he not very well have been tampering with Russia's relations to France? On the other hand it may be urged that Russia was perhaps only playing the part of a prudent and sober friend who refused to allow France to engage in a deadly conflict over issues that were not vital. It is likely, however, that Russia's attitude need not be accounted for either in treachery or in a wise concern for the best interests of France, but rather in the terms of her alliance with France.

The Dual Alliance was, of course, directed in the first instance rather against the Triple Alliance than against Great Britain. The letters exchanged between de Giers and Ribot in August, 1891, establishing the Franco-Russian alliance did not, it is true, specify a prospective enemy.[21] But the military convention,

[20] *British Documents,* I, No. 59, p. 38, Scott to Salisbury, November 2, 1898.

[21] *Documents Diplomatiques: L'alliance franco-russe,* No. 17, Annexe, p. 16, Giers to Mohrenheim, August 21, 1891.

which later gave practical effect to the alliance, mentioned by name Germany, Austria, and Italy; and its sixth article runs, "La présente Convention aura la même durée que la Triple Alliance."[22] When subsequently, in 1899, Delcassé wished to alter the terms and import of the convention, the fault he found with it was precisely that its existence depended too explicitly upon the duration of the Triple Alliance: "Née de la Triple Alliance, elle s'evanouirait avec elle."[23]

No doubt Great Britain, too, was in the minds of the negotiators of the convention; she was even spoken of between them as a potential adherent of the opposing Triple Alliance.[24] The British themselves were not sure how they stood toward the Dual Alliance, for it will be remembered that the exact terms of the treaty were still a secret. During the Fashoda crisis, therefore, the British seem to have had some small qualms. Sir Horace Rumbold asked the German ambassador in Vienna if he believed there was an arrangement or treaty between France and Russia regarding a case of war with England.[25] But in general both the government and the people of Great Britain had their minds at rest on that score. And it is difficult to adopt the view sometimes expressed that by the time at which we

[22] *Ibid.*, No. 71, p. 92, General Boisdeffre to French minister of war, August 18, 1892.

[23] *Ibid.*, No. 95, p. 131, Delcassé to Loubet, August 12, 1899.

[24] *Ibid.*, No. 3, p. 3, Laboulaye to Ribot, July 18, 1891.

[25] *G.P.*, XIV, 3921, p. 400, Eulenburg to Hohenlohe, December 12, 1898; *British Documents,* I, No. 123, p. 102, Rumbold to Salisbury, December 5.

have arrived (1898) the Franco-Russian alliance had been diverted from its original object, and was now virtually a league against Great Britain. The conduct of Russia over Fashoda should be presumptive evidence to the contrary; so, too, the conduct of France in the Near East a year earlier, when Hanotaux had endeavored throughout the Cretan question to avoid being compelled to choose between England and Russia.[26]

It cannot be denied, however, that indirectly at least the alliance turned out to be a mainspring of hostilities against the British empire. It induced in both France and Russia a bolder spirit, and redoubled the pressure they could exert upon the common adversary in Asia and Africa. But the Dual Alliance as such was not designed as an engine against British imperialism. It tended rather to restore that Continental balance so much desired by Great Britain, and although the treaty had remained unpublished, yet there was evidence that it referred only to the European situation, and did not contemplate common action outside of Europe—at least, no action so drastic as war.

The idea of a coalition of the whole Continent against England seems to have commended itself at one time to Count Muravieff.[27] But a coalition that would include both France and Germany could not have found much favor in either quarter. And, at any

[26] *G.P.*, XIII, No. 3435, p. 72, Radolin to Hohenlohe, July 4, 1897.

[27] *Ibid.*, XIII, No. 3427, p. 63, Hohenlohe to Radolin, February 1, 1897.

rate, no coalition yet existed, and in the present case the British had shrewdly assumed that they would be dealing with France alone. Events were to prove the assumption correct.

Whether, therefore, the Czar and his ministers were shirking a treaty obligation, or were simply standing coolly on the strict letter of their bargain, it all came to the same thing: Russia's friendship was not so disinterested that she would risk anything against England in the Fashoda quarrel. That and no more was the worth of the Russian Alliance in a French colonial dispute. In *revanche*, however, there might be some reasonable expectation of turning the alliance to a better account. *Revanche* was another matter.

The fundamental idea of the Franco-Russian alliance would seem to have been mutual protection against Germany and the Triple Alliance; and therefore it could be looked upon as formally pacific. But measures of precaution against Germany could not fail also to assume somewhat the character of hostile designs; defense would merge into offense. Thus there were two possible ways of regarding the Dual Alliance.

From the very first the French were disposed to take for granted that the alliance would serve the ends of *revanche;* and that assumption unquestionably underlay the popular enthusiasm which the entente of Kronstadt evoked.[28] There is evidence that Germany also held the same view. In the year after the Kron-

[28] Débidour, *Hist. Dipl.,* I, 177 ff.

stadt celebrations there took place the largest in-
crease of the German army since the foundation of
the empire. The German Emperor never ceased to look
upon the Franco-Russian union with suspicion. He
once told Prince Lobanoff (1895) that if France and
Russia wished to make war he could not prevent it,
and that he was forced to regard the "constant celebrations and speeches, as well as the official and unof-
ficial visits exchanged between Paris and St. Petersburg as significant symptoms which could not be ignored."[29] And he had used these rather threatening
words in spite of the fact that Lobanoff had come to
Berlin on a friendly visit, and had brought with him
assurances of the peaceful intentions of France and
Russia.

It was known, of course, that Russian opinion was
generally very favorable to France. The Russian government regarded France as a useful diplomatic and
financial *appoint*. The masses cherished for the French
a sort of sentimental attachment which had a certain
moral if not political significance. And there was also
a small but active group which loved the republic in
France, and sought to exploit the Franco-Russian relations in the interests of liberal government in Russia.[30] As toward Germany, however, Russia had always been inclined to deprecate the idea of hostility;
and in the very beginning the Czar had made it clear
that the Russian government could not countenance

[29] *The Kaiser's Memoirs*, p. 61.

[30] *G.P.*, XIII, No. 3444, p. 82, Bülow to Eulenburg, August
20, 1897.

schemes of *revanche*. In an audience with Montebello (December 17, 1893) he had admitted the validity of French patriotic sentiment over the lost provinces; but he had added that "entre ce sentiment trop naturel et l'idée d'une provocation pour arriver à le realizer, d'une revanche en un mot, il y a loin."[31] Nevertheless, the French seem to have been a little blind to the facts, and to have long persisted in the belief that the alliance could be made somehow to minister to *revanche*.

Disillusionment came only slowly, but it came inevitably. In the months that preceded the Fashoda crisis it seemed to Münster that France was more and more awakening out of its dreams of revenge—dreams in which Russia stood as the avenging angel for Alsace-Lorraine. A war between Russia and Germany could no longer be counted on; and without Russia's help neither the republic nor the army wanted war with Germany.[32] The lower classes and the provinces still held to their faith in the Russian alliance. But Paris was too well informed to continue in its credulity. The feeling was growing that France had cast herself too incontinently into the arms of Russia; that she had made all the sacrifices required, and that requital was wanting. Thus, wrote Münster sententiously, are dissolved the bonds of love.[33]

But while the relations with Russia were growing

[31] *Documents Diplomatiques: L'alliance franco-russe*, No. 90, p. 125, Montebello to Casimir-Perier, December 17, 1893.

[32] *G.P.*, XIII, No. 3430, p. 66, Münster to Hohenlohe, February 3, 1897.

[33] *Ibid.*, XIII, No. 3432, p. 68, Münster to Hohenlohe, April 7, 1897.

less secure, yet the fact could not be safely revealed or admitted. Even at home the position of the French government was growing very difficult. Of Hanotaux they said in Paris, "Il fait tout pour les Russes, et rien pour la France."[34] He was much blamed for having sacrificed French independence to Russia. Münster compared him to the captain of a ship in tow, who is not at all sure where he is to be taken, and yet who does not quite dare to cut himself adrift.[35] The French government sought, therefore, by some conspicuous gesture to save what was left of the Russian alliance, and if possible to rehabilitate it. To that end President Faure proposed to pay a visit of ceremony to St. Petersburg during the summer of 1897, the pretext being to make a return for the Czar's visit to France in 1896.

The President's excursion met some opposition in France, since the Franco-Russian alliance was losing a good deal of its power of enchantment in French minds.[36] The Russians, too, may have awaited his coming without much warmth of expectancy. Witte exclaimed in mock dismay to the German ambassador, "Was in aller Welt soll man mit ihm drei Tage lang machen!"[37] But outwardly, at least, M. Faure, who

[34] *Ibid.*, XIII, No. 3430, p. 65, Münster to Hohenlohe, February 3, 1897.

[35] *Ibid.*, XIII, No. 3431, p. 67, Münster to Hohenlohe, February 21, 1897.

[36] *Ibid.*, XIII, No. 3434, p. 71, Münster to Hohenlohe, July 3, 1897.

[37] *Ibid.*, XIII, No. 3433, p. 70, Radolin to Hohenlohe, May 31, 1897.

was accompanied by M. Hanotaux, was well received, and the journals were active in stirring up enthusiasm. For, as Prince Radolin reported to the German government, no politically intelligent Russian would think of giving up the friendship of France when it could be had so cheaply as with toasts and parades.[38]

Once they were in St. Petersburg, however (August 23–27, 1897), Faure and Hanotaux were successful beyond expectation. To Radolin it was painfully evident that from hour to hour the Czar grew warmer toward his guests; the farewells were much more cordial than the greetings. And quite naturally Radolin lamented the Czar's friendliness which he set down to infirmity of character.[39] And, indeed, before they went away the Frenchmen achieved an astonishing stroke in diplomacy. At a farewell breakfast on board the "Pothuau," they enticed from the Czar a most important declaration in which fell the significant words, "Nos deux nations amies et alliées."[40]

The French government was immensely gratified by this public avowal. Theretofore French ministers who had in the Chambre spoken of the Russian entente had been accustomed to have their statements met with incredulity and derision. It was now hoped that the Czar's affirmation would be believed. Nevertheless, there seems to have been some lingering skepticism.

[38] *Ibid.,* XIII, No. 3436, p. 73, Radolin to Hohenlohe, July 14, 1897.

[39] *Ibid.,* XIII, No. 3447, p. 85, Radolin to Hohenlohe, August 28, 1897.

[40] *Ibid.,* XIII, No. 3445, p. 83, Radolin to Foreign Office, August 27, 1897.

The German chargé Müller heard in Paris that in the judgment of financial and other well-informed circles nothing was changed in the relations of France and Russia.[41] Some persons doubted even the fact of an alliance. A French politician said to Münster, "Tout cela n'est que phrase, on n'a pas fait usage d'encre et de plumes."[42] And in any case the cult of the Russian alliance seemed to be on the wane, whether it rested on agreement by word of mouth or on written treaty. Even Russia's ordinary loyalty toward France was beginning to be called in question.

The French government was, of course, ignorant of what went on confidentially between Russia and Germany, but appearances were not reassuring. Just before Faure's visit to Russia, and in the same month of August, 1897, the German Emperor had also met the Czar at Peterhof. He was accompanied by Hohenlohe and Bülow. Views were exchanged. Bülow wrote back to the Foreign Office that while Muravieff and Witte still wished, no doubt, to maintain the present intimate relations with France, which were economically and diplomatically useful to Russia, yet it was his impression that their enthusiasm for France was cooling.[43] And Radolin averred that the fable of the injury done to Russia at the Congress of Berlin, which

[41] *Ibid.*, XIII, No. 3449, p. 86, Müller to Foreign Office, August 30, 1897.

[42] *Ibid.*, XIII, No. 3450, p. 87, Münster to Hohenlohe, October 5, 1897.

[43] *Ibid.*, XIII, No. 3438, p. 76, Bülow to Foreign Office, August 10, 1897.

had always haunted the muddled Russian heads *(in den unklaren russischen Köpfen spukte)* was being replaced by a doctrine of community of interests between Russia and Germany. And he believed that it had been made manifest anew that Russia in her own interests, and so long as Germany kept her sword sharp, would and must seek union with the German empire.[44]

Also the German Emperor exerted a marked personal influence in Russia, even if he did not while in St. Petersburg excite the universal admiration which Radolin thought he observed. His keen conversation, his assumption of authority, and his martial bearing would naturally strike a contrast with the mild and irresolute courses of the Czar. The Kaiser's habitual influence over the Czar was undoubted, although the French could not have known its full measure. Ever since the Czar's accession in 1894 the Emperor William had not ceased by suggestion and by open admonition to cover with his own ideas that "page with no writing on it." He corresponded with the Czar "openly and without backthought," and he made no effort to conceal his aversion for Russia's alliance with France: "If you are allied for better, for worse with the French, well then keep those damned rascals in order and make them sit still."[45] Or again, and with prodigious solemnity, "Nicky, take my word on it, the curse of God has stricken those people [the French]

[44] *Ibid.,* XIII, No. 3443, p. 80, Radolin to Hohenlohe, August 18, 1897.

[45] *Kaiser's Letters,* p. 22.

forever "[46] And in November of 1898 he wrote sneeringly of the Czar's "friends and allies," and referred to their foolish step in evacuating Fashoda.[47]

It is improbable, however, that the personal ascendancy of the German Emperor over the Czar by itself determined the conduct of the Russian government during the Fashoda crisis. But it is also reasonable to suppose that whatever influence the Kaiser might have wielded would not be on the side of Russian intervention. On October 28 he wrote from Jaffa suggesting an exchange of views.[48] His question, "How do you look at the situation?" seems to imply a willingness to act in accord with Russia. And that supposition is strengthened by the contents of another letter dated a fortnight later (though never actually dispatched in its original wording), in which he wrote, "I am bound to take my precautions and want to conform my politics as far as possible to Yours in case difficulties should arise."[49] Now although earlier in the same letter he had referred to the Bahr-el-Ghazelle as belonging rightfully to France, yet it is difficult to suppose that he would have conformed his politics to the Czar's had that course entailed supporting France against England. A more plausible conjecture is that he hoped by persistent intimacies to inject his own

[46] *Ibid.,* p. 25.

[47] *Ibid.,* p. 69.

[48] *G.P.,* XIV, No. 3900, p. 382, Bülow to Foreign Office, October 28, 1898.

[49] *Ibid.,* XIV, No. 3913, p. 395, Bülow to Foreign Office (Kaiser to Czar), November 11, 1898.

policy into the mind of the Czar Nicholas; in short,
that he was tampering with the Franco-Russian alliance.

It is not likely that the Russians were yet prepared
to close with Germany in a formal entente even had the
offer been made. For when in the early summer of 1898
the British were making overtures to Germany, and
when the Emperor in turn had made a rather unbecom-
ing offer to the Czar to accept bids from Russia, too,[50]
the Czar had declined with a somewhat frigid dignity.[51]
But it also seems evident that the Russians did not sufficiently repel German insinuations. It is a question
whether the Czar's own chief ministers were attached
with full constancy and singleness of heart to the
French alliance. At least in some of their casual utterances there was lacking the tone of complete loyalty. Sometimes they seemed disposed to make light of
the French nation and to represent the alliance as a
sort of condescension toward France taken in the interests of the peace of Europe. Lobanoff had once
(September, 1896) said to Hohenlohe that Russia had
"really done Europe a great service by taking up
France. Goodness knows what these people might have

[50] *Kaiser's Letters,* pp. 54–55, "Now as my old and trusted
friend I beg you to tell me what you can offer me and will do if
I refuse [the British offer]."

[51] *G.P.,* XIV, No. 3803, p. 250, Czar to Kaiser:
"It is very difficult for me, if not quite impossible, to answer
your question whether it is useful or not for Germany to accept
these often repeated english *(sic)* proposals, as I have not the
slightest knowledge of their value. You must of course decide
what is best and most necessary for your country."

taken it into their heads to do if we did not keep them in check."[52] More recently (January, 1897) Muravieff had assured Marschall that the Franco-Russian entente had an entirely peaceful object; that Russian policy would never think of supporting French chauvinism against Germany; and that he did not for a moment contemplate a divergence in politics between Russia and Germany.[53] Still later during an audience with the Kaiser, in which he "overflowed with courtesy, obligingness, and assurances of friendship," Muravieff had offered discreetly to act as a sort of intermediary between France and Germany whenever his services might be useful.[54]

The French were, of course, kept in ignorance of these things. But they could not have failed to observe that Russian diplomacy had adopted a mood of too great impartiality as between Germany and France. In affairs outside of Europe the Germans seemed to be in even closer co-operation with Russia than were the French themselves. In the Near Eastern troubles of 1897 Count Muravieff inclined to the German attitude of tolerance for the *status quo* in Turkey, and would give the French government no assurances regarding the regulation of Turkish finance which above all concerned France. During the Kaiser's visit to St. Petersburg (August, 1897) Muravieff had declared that in

[52] Hohenlohe, *Memoirs,* II, 478.

[53] *G.P.,* XIII, No. 3426, p. 61, memorandum by Marschall, January 31, 1897.

[54] *Ibid.,* XIII, No. 3428, p. 64, Kaiser to Hohenlohe, February 1, 1897.

the matter of Turkish reforms Russia and Germany must stand against France and England.[55] Moreover, Russia and Austria had recently come to an agreement in the Balkans.[56] Lord Salisbury had grumbled against it as damaging to British relations with the Triple Alliance; and it must certainly have caused even greater suspicion and dissatisfaction in France.[57] In the Far East, too, Russia and Germany had for some years seemed disposed to co-operate. Under German incitements Russia had been pressing her interests in China and growing steadily less attentive to purely European affairs. About the year 1897 Russia was ready to recognize as legitimate Germany's desire for a naval base on the China coast;[58] and the Emperor records in his *Memoirs* that at that time "it was particularly necessary not to interfere with Russia's designs, nor to disturb her."[59] They became accomplices. And after their successful seizures in China, the Kaiser exulted in the thought that "we two will make a good pair of sentinels at the entrance of the Gulf of Petchili."[60] France must have looked on with a

[55] *Ibid.*, XIII, No. 3429, p. 64, Kaiser to Eulenburg, February 3, 1897; No. 3430, p. 66, Münster to Hohenlohe, February 3, 1897; No. 3438, p. 76, Bülow to Foreign Office, August 10, 1897.

[56] Pribram, *The Secret Treaties of Austria-Hungary, 1879–1914*, I, 184 ff.

[57] *G.P.*, XIV, No. 3797, p. 234, Hatzfeldt to Foreign Office, May 15, 1898.

[58] *Ibid.*, XIII, No. 3426, p. 59, memorandum by Marschall, January 31, 1897.

[59] *The Kaiser's Memoirs*, p. 65.

[60] *Kaiser's Letters*, p. 46; cf. also *G.P.*, XIV, No. 3733, p. 121, and No. 3734, p. 122.

good deal of concern while her chief enemy consorted so comfortably with her only ally.

Thus in *revanche* as in colonies the Russian alliance seemed to be falling short of reasonable expectations. Russia was deep in her own concerns. The Russian ministers seemed to look quite dispassionately and with a sort of cold realism upon the alliance. Where it served, they would use it; but in Russia's relations with Germany it was as often as not an inconvenience, and was therefore likely to be ignored or depreciated. Germany was allowed to believe, indeed had been asked to believe, that Russia would never permit the alliance to become an instrument of *revanche*. Perhaps France could not justly complain of her ally; perhaps she had miscalculated her own position under the treaty. But it is certain that she had hoped for much from the Russian alliance and was getting little. In the present instance France required, as also she may have expected, more than a perfunctory support from Russia. For if Germany's simple neutrality was to be accounted a menace, then the Russian alliance offered no security. And Russia, who was ostentatiously neutral as between France and England, could have asked of Germany no more than neutrality.

To sum up the whole argument then: France abandoned Fashoda for reasons which do not appear in the diplomatic correspondence with Great Britain. Nor is it likely that she was much moved by consideration of her presumptive military or naval inequality with Great Britain, nor by the distractions of her domestic turmoils. Her real reasons may, however, be divined through an examination of her situation in Europe.

French policy was always being pulled about between two almost irreconcilable motives. Desire for colonial expansion took her into Africa and Asia, and made of her a rival to British imperialism. Desire for reinstatement in Europe and for revenge upon Germany prompted her to withdraw her energies from distant enterprises. But whichever of these she chose to regard as of first importance, she could never ignore the other. If she expended herself without reserve upon colonies, the German enmity might become dangerously insistent. If she made a point of *revanche*, then her colonies were left to the mercies of Great Britain, the devourer of territory.

In the case of Fashoda, a policy of expansion had led inevitably to a clash with Great Britain. But a serious quarrel with Great Britain over colonies called for precautions against Germany. Hanotaux had seen it, and had striven for good relations or even an entente with Germany. He had failed, however, to find a proper occasion; and when the matter fell into the hands of Delcassé it was already too late to make good the deficiency. To make matters worse, the late rivalries between Germany and Great Britain seemed to be on the point of solution, and already the two powers had come to a partial accord in Africa.

But it is at least conceivable that France might have made head against Great Britain and have been secured against Germany had the Russian alliance brought her any effectual support in either direction.

In the crisis, however, Russia declined to support France against Great Britain, as no doubt she had strictly a right to do; and Russia's ambiguous relations with Germany left France exposed and impotent against her traditional enemy in Europe.

Therefore, whereas for Great Britain the Fashoda issue resolved itself into a simple question of empire in Africa, for France it was inevitably involved with other calculations of the balance of power in Europe. Great Britain faced a single hostile front, while France faced two. In dealing with Great Britain France had also to guard her flank against Germany and the Triple Alliance. There lay her principal weakness. And the Russian alliance upon which she might have relied for support (in Europe if not in Africa) proved in the event to be little better than a platonic association without validity in the present exigency.

CHAPTER X

THE SEQUEL

With March 21, 1899, the Fashoda incident was formally closed. But bygones were not to be easily or immediately dismissed between France and Great Britain. France very naturally smarted under defeat. There was scarcely any way to conceal or alleviate the hurt to her pride. She had avoided war, but not without seeming to shuffle and waver in the face of its perils; and she had been humiliated almost as completely and conspicuously as if the British fleet had steamed into Brest or Toulon and summoned her to submit. Delcassé himself must have felt the bitterness of the moment, and he did not entirely repress his indignation: "Ils me font avaler un crapaud par jour et ça ne finit pas et ne finira jamais."[1] In the summer of 1899, and when the settlement of March 21 was already nearly six months old, he complained over again to Monson of what he regarded as England's habitual *mauvais vouloir* against France; and before he could recover his usual geniality, he flung out petulantly that he began to believe the politicians were right who argued that there was nothing to be done with England.[2] French public opinion, too, gave vent to an

[1] *Grosse Politik,* XIII, No. 3558, p. 252, memorandum by correspondent of *Kölnische Zeitung,* December 5, 1898.

[2] *British Documents,* I, No. 259, p. 212, Monson to Salisbury, August 14, 1899.

ill-humour that was not always seemly. A newspaper declared resentfully, "We offered Lord Salisbury Fashoda and our friendship, and he replied that he only wanted Fashoda."[3] The French journals railed angrily against Great Britain, and the attacks sometimes degenerated into purposeless scurrility. They went even beyond decency in caricaturing Britain's venerable queen. Chamberlain declared (November 3, 1899) that it was "an abuse which has been carried to an extreme which I do not think has been witnessed for generations."[4]

Great Britain, on its part, remained stiffly resentful under the memory of the late dispute and under these fresh evidences of French hostility. The "pinpricks" were stabbing almost too deeply to be ignored. The British believed that they had already shown unexampled patience under incessant provocation. Even members of the cabinet were ready to advocate that an end be made of a contentious neighbor's power to disturb the peace of the empire. The *Daily Mail* incited the nation to a bullying vindictiveness, and recommended a policy that should deliberately exploit the Fashoda triumph against the French in all parts of the world whatsoever.[5] Münster, in Paris, believed that England was only waiting until her naval preparations were complete (say after 1900) to deal finally with France; and the Kaiser, in his marginal, contra-

[3] "France, Russia and the Nile," *Cont. Rev.,* LXXIV, 761.

[4] *Liberal Magazine,* VII (1899), 593.

[5] Lowes-Dickinson, *The International Anarchy, 1904–1914,* p. 42.

dicted not the imputation of malevolence in England, but only Münster's assertion that France would passively await attack. France and Russia, he thought, would immediately begin to build ships.[6] Perhaps the Germans were too ready to believe the worst; but it is at least certain that there was ill-feeling on both sides, and that a settlement of the Fashoda question did not imply a reconciliation.

It happened, moreover, that just a few weeks after the Fashoda negotiations were resumed in the winter of 1899, but before the settlement, there broke over the two powers another small controversial squall which, although it ran its course in two months, was almost the Fashoda incident over again in miniature. While Hanotaux was still in office the French government had obtained from the Sultan of Muscat a concession for a coaling-station in the Persian Gulf. The French did not immediately avail themselves of the privilege. But in February, 1899, the warship "Scorpion" visited Muscat, and the arrangement with the Sultan was made public. Thereupon the British Resident summoned the three British warships stationed in the gulf in order to prevent by force, if necessary, the fulfilment of the French concession and the hoisting of the French flag. The Sultan of Muscat, under threat of an English bombardment, withdrew his concession, and the French had no recourse but to vain protest. M. Cambon remonstrated with Lord Salisbury against the "excessive action" of the British admiral, and thought the British view of the case "need not have

[6] *G.P.,* XIV, No. 3944, p. 425, marginal.

been asserted by a threat of bombardment." Salisbury replied that in the matter of sentiment the French government had perhaps a grievance, but in the matter of substance the British action was entirely right. But Cambon persisted: If France were willing to declare her innocent intentions, might not some provision be made for a French coaling-station? To which Salisbury answered that the matter really rested with the India Office, and so avoided giving an immediate refusal.[7] Subsequently, however, he explained not unreasonably that if it had been only a question of the French keeping coal-stores at Muscat, the British would have been glad to meet their wishes; but that a cession or lease of territory was another matter. Delcassé (who unlike his predecessor was abundantly even-tempered) could not altogether hide his chagrin and irritation. Thus again France had attempted to dispute a British territorial monopoly, and again her theoretical rights had been met by the solid fact of British predominance within the territories in question. And Russia also in this as in the Fashoda case had refused support, although she was herself deeply interested in the Persian Gulf. Count Muravieff was said to be quite calm over the Anglo-French disagreements at Muscat, and to be confident that there would be no unpleasant consequences; for which disloyalty (if it was indeed that), he perhaps deserved the Kaiser's sarcasm, "Ein merkwürdiger Allierter!"[8]

[7] *British Documents,* I, No. 255, pp. 209–10, Salisbury to Monson, February 22, 1899.

[8] *G.P.,* XIV, Nos. 3934–39, No. 3938, p. 419, marginal.

Relations between Great Britain and France could hardly have been worse, therefore, short of an actual conflict of arms. The future was, of course, hidden from both; and probably both would have been incredulous over the idea of an entente within five years. There was scarcely the faintest premonition of so momentous a revolution in affairs. Yet from these unpromising beginnings in the spring of 1899 France and Great Britain were destined to advance steadily toward the epochal conventions of 1904; and by reading backward through those crowded years it is now possible to make out the first almost imperceptible pause and turn for the better in Anglo-French relations.

One of the earliest and most auspicious symptoms of change was that these two powers, each on its own side, had begun to feel dissatisfaction with the habitual courses and affinities in diplomacy.

For some time Great Britain continued to court Germany, and there is evidence that Germany was by no means impervious to British solicitations. Toward the end of the negotiations over the Portuguese colonies in the summer of 1898 the German Foreign Office had written to Hatzfeldt that the British government should be given to understand that the agreement in South Africa was regarded in Germany as a point of departure for further co-operation with England, and that Germany had been at some pains not to bind herself in any other direction.[9] But within a month the

[9] *Ibid.*, XIV, No. 3856, p. 323, Richthofen to Hatzfeldt, August 20, 1898; *British Documents,* I, No. 85, p. 67, Balfour to Lascelles, August 19, 1898.

Fashoda crisis intervened, and no further progress had been made toward a general understanding.

After the crisis the German government took credit in England for having at least refrained from interference. They argued that their attitude of reserve during the controversy was an evidence of friendliness; had they wished they might have effected a *rapprochement* with France and her allies, and in that case Great Britain would not have found in Paris the same disposition to yield.[10] It seems a very questionable sort of friendliness, however; and besides, if the German government did not wish to see France and England go to war over Fashoda, it can hardly be supposed that they were prompted by friendliness toward England. On the contrary, being convinced that such a war would end in the defeat and spoliation of France, they hoped for a peaceful settlement, not out of regard for either France or England, but because they feared that after the downfall of France an overmighty England would be more than ever a standing menace to German enterprises overseas.[11]

Nevertheless, it is evident that Germany was anxious to avoid a definite break with England. While France and Great Britain were in disagreement over affairs in the Persian Gulf during the spring of 1899, a German agent drew the attention of his government also to the possibility of securing a harbor and pro-

[10] *Ibid.,* XIV, No. 3945, p. 426, Hatzfeldt to Hohenlohe, June 30, 1899.

[11] *Ibid.,* XIV, No. 3909, p. 391, C.-Rudenhausen to Hohenlohe, November 8, 1898.

tectorate in Muscat. It was desirable, he argued, to have an eastern water-terminus for the projected railway, and Koweit was suggested as also suitable for a German coaling-station. But Bülow disapproved of the scheme from the first, on the ground that Great Britain's long domination in the Gulf could not be infringed without endangering Anglo-German relations.[12]

Great Britain on her side seems to have been quite prepared to make a friend of Germany even at the price of concessions. In Turkey the British professed themselves ready to acquiesce in Germany's ascendancy. The *Times* declared that there was no power to which England would more gladly surrender the Turkish railway enterprises than to Germany (November, 1899). Other newspapers concurred, solacing themselves with the thought that at any rate Russia would be bilked.[13] Cecil Rhodes, in an interview with the Kaiser, urged that Germany undertake to build the Bagdad Railway and open up Mesopotamia, a project which he seemed perfectly willing to trade off for his cherished Cape-to-Cairo railway scheme.[14] Moreover, Great Britain found it prudent now to meet Germany's persistent demands for a partition of the Samoan Islands. It was a matter upon which the Germans had

[12] *Ibid.*, XIV, No. 3996, pp. 509 ff. Bülow to Kaiser, February 2, 1899.

[13] *Ibid.*, XIV, No. 3995, p. 506, Hatzfeldt to Hohenlohe, November 30, 1899.

[14] *The Kaiser's Memoirs,* pp. 87–89; cf. Eckardstein, *Ten Years at the Court of St. James,* pp. 102–3.

always shown an unaccountable keenness. Hatzfeldt had been pursuing the negotiations in London with extraordinary pertinacity and even vehemence, but without much apparent success. In November, however, the Emperor actually threatened to abandon his proposed visit to England if there should be no settlement of Samoa; and Colonel Grierson, who reported the conversation with his majesty, thought that this time he might be in earnest.[15] On November 14, therefore, a convention was signed which gave Germany all she could have expected in Samoa, besides effecting some minor arrangements in Zanzibar and West Africa,[16] a termination of the affair which was received in Germany with triumphant satisfaction.

A few days after the Samoan settlement, the German Emperor with Bülow came to England; and Chamberlain seized the occasion to elicit from the German Foreign Secretary his informal consent to a project for an Anglo-German entente. Relying upon these private commitments, Chamberlain almost immediately proclaimed the new policy in his celebrated speech at Leicester (November 30), in which he drew attention to the "natural alliance" between Germany and the great Anglo-Saxon peoples.[17] The *Times* doubted the wisdom of so abrupt a *démarche*: "Our German friends are no doubt surprised at finding the relations of

[15] *British Documents,* I, No. 154, p. 130, Grierson to Gough, November 6, 1899; cf. Eckardstein, *op. cit.,* p. 118.

[16] *G.P.,* XIV, No. 4115, pp. 671–72, Hatzfeldt to Salisbury, October 27, 1899.

[17] *Liberal Magazine,* VII (1899), 576.

Great Britain with Germany described with an effusion for which no authoritative utterance in their own country has prepared them in the smallest degree."[18] And, indeed, it was an error; the headlong Chamberlain had gone too fast. Holstein, the renowned "councilor" of the German Foreign Office, who disliked and mistrusted Great Britain, had already laid it down authoritatively in one of his long memoranda (April, 1899) that Germany could make no use of an alliance of the "three Anglo-Saxon peoples" which had been lately proposed in England as a sort of law of nature.[19] Bülow himself had not the hardihood to withstand public opinion in Germany; and the policy of an English alliance was publicly repudiated.

Thus closed, not the last chance, but the last favorable chance of an Anglo-German alliance. A year before, and on the eve of the Fashoda crisis, Bülow had expressed a conviction that relations with England would become either much better or much worse, that they stood at the forks.[20] And now in the autumn of 1899 apparently the wrong turning had been taken. Bülow explains his course as based, first, on mistrust of England who, he was convinced, would disregard the stipulations of any treaty which proved inconvenient; and, second, on his fear that Germany would

[18] *Times,* December 2, 1899.

[19] *G.P.,* XIV, No. 4016, p. 535, memorandum by Holstein, April 17, 1899.

[20] *Ibid.,* XIV, No. 3857, p. 324, Bülow to Foreign Office, August 20, 1898.

be made a cat's paw against Russia in Asia.[21] Moreover, in his mind, as also in the German Emperor's,
there was awakening a profound jealousy of British
sea-power, and especially since German impotence had
been revealed in the South African troubles of 1896.
To the Kaiser it had not ceased to be a matter of bitter
regret that in that year Germany's fleet as compared
to England's was as naught—"einer Hand voll Erbsen
gleich zu erachten ist."[22] Both Emperor and Minister
now suspected Great Britain of a design to hamper
the German naval program through an alliance.[23]
And besides, the German government was beginning to
regard freedom of action as of more importance than
security through alliances. They felt themselves already strong enough for wholly independent courses.
Hatzfeldt wrote confidently from London that neither
of the great opposing groups in Europe could then do
anything without first making sure of Germany; that
the time was approaching when they must all seek Germany's friendship, and upon her own terms.[24]

Meanwhile, however, there was no deliberate intention to alienate Great Britain. Before Fashoda the
Kaiser had written to the German Foreign Office some
observations of his own upon the inconveniences of a

[21] Bülow, *Imperial Germany*, p. 32.

[22] *G.P.*, XIII, No. 3396, p. 4, Kaiser to Hohenlohe, October
25, 1896; Seymour, *Diplomatic Background of the World War*,
pp. 92 ff.

[23] Bülow, *Imperial Germany*, p. 32; *G.P.*, XIV, No. 3799,
p. 239.

[24] *G.P.*, XIV, No. 4019, p. 544, Hatzfeldt to Foreign Office,
May 1, 1899.

rapprochement with Great Britain; but he had added that it was most important to keep official sentiment in England favorable to Germany and hopeful
—as otherwise it might turn suddenly away toward
France.[25] But by the end of 1899 British hopes had
been kept too long on the stretch. And when the South
African war broke out, and German public opinion
grew vociferous against Great Britain, and the Kaiser
in spite of all his efforts was unable to clear himself of
imputations of hostile intrigue,[26] then Great Britain
reluctantly but definitely began to relinquish the idea
of an understanding with Germany, and to fasten her
thoughts upon new allurements in diplomacy. From
the discomforts of isolation in Europe Great Britain
had had but two possible lines of escape: one toward
the Triple Alliance and the other toward the Dual Alliance. There was no third alternative. And since Germany seemed disposed to close one path against her, it
was only natural that she should turn to explore the
other.

As for France, it was to be expected that in the
first recoil from the shock of the Fashoda defeat, she
should have fallen into momentary oblivion of her hatred of Germany. In November, 1898, a correspondent
of the *Kölnische Zeitung* made a journey to Paris,
where at a breakfast arranged by M. Hansen, a confidential agent of the French government, he met a company of men who were then serving in the French Foreign Office. He found their sentiments strongly colored

[25] *Ibid.,* XIV, No. 3790, p. 217, Kaiser to Foreign Office,
April 10, 1898.

[26] *The Kaiser's Memoirs,* p. 86.

by aversion for Great Britain, and they talked even of reconciliation with Germany. The idea of *revanche*, they said, was beginning to wane in France. As for colonies, France had as many as she needed; therefore, she would regard with favor Germany's colonial expansion, and especially in China. Every colony won by Germany was thereby saved from falling into the hands of England. The same correspondent found Delcassé filled with indignation over the treatment to which England had subjected him. He intimated that *rapprochement* with Germany was his most serious aim. He did not once utter the word "alliance," but he said that thenceforth France and Germany must follow a common policy: "Il faut refaire la politique suivie depuis seize ans." His German interviewer then suggested that there would be difficulty in finding a French ministry with enough courage to make that proposal before the Chambre; to which Delcassé immediately retorted, "J'y irai demain, si vous voulez!" And he ended with a wish that in Germany they might be persuaded that he and a majority of Frenchmen were striving for a reconciliation with Germany.[27]

A few weeks later two German warships put in at Algiers. The officers and men were well received by the French authorities, and the Germans on their part made an excellent impression. A rumor was spread that the German ships had been dispatched to support France in an eventual war with England.[28] The Ger-

[27] *G.P.*, XIII, No. 3558, p. 252–53, Hohn of the *Kölnische Zeitung,* December 5, 1898.

[28] *Ibid.,* XIII, No. 3563, p. 252, Consul Goetsch to Hohenlohe, February 10, 1899.

man Emperor was moved to send a message of thanks to the French President for the reception accorded his ships, and intimated that he was about to confer decorations upon the French officers who participated in the courtesies at Algiers.[29] When President Faure expressed a wish to meet the Emperor in person, Münster was instructed to reply in polite though prudently vague terms.[30]

These passages and sentiments may have been without practical consequences in politics; but it is at least notable that in the early spring of 1899 the Franco-German economic rivalries in Turkey were greatly allayed by important compromises and arrangements between the Deutsche Bank and the Ottoman Bank.[31] And in urging upon the French a financial accord with the Germans in Constantinople, Marschall did not fail to take his text from the late unfortunate experiences of the French at Fashoda.[32]

In France, however, these novel humors could not have had much depth of root, and the summer of good will toward Germany was too short to bear fruit in any abundance. When in July the German Emperor made a complimentary visit to the French school-ship "Iphigénie" at Bergen, his courteous intentions somehow

[29] Ibid., XIII, No. 3565, p. 263, Bülow to Münster, February 20, 1899.

[30] Ibid., XIII, No. 3564, p. 263, Bülow to Münster, February 11, 1899.

[31] Earle, Turkey, the Great Powers, and the Bagdad Railway, p. 59.

[32] G.P., XIV, No. 3983, p. 481, Marschall to Foreign Office, April 12, 1899.

failed to make their calculated impression in France. The event received a bad press in Paris.[33] France seemed to be already reverted to her habitual mood. Most of the newspapers were refusing to entertain the idea of an entente with Germany as being contrary to the interests and honor of France. And when a little later the Kaiser proposed to lay a wreath of laurel upon a French grave on the battle-field of St. Privat (during the ceremonies of unveiling a memorial to a German regiment), he was advised by Münster from Paris that his friendly gesture would not be understood or appreciated in France.[34]

And, indeed, the idea of a Franco-German alliance directed against Great Britain was a sort of political naïveté. The revulsion of French feeling had been too sudden to endure; and on the side of Germany, while they were naturally ready to make the most out of the situation, yet they were moved by calculation rather than by sentiment. It is hardly to be supposed that they would be at once carried out of their considered courses. Bülow wrote in a memorandum that Germany might regard hopefully but without illusion the French attempts at reconciliation; that, in fact, they might look upon it as simply a project to employ Germany's power for the overthrow of France's colonial rival, while at the same time France

[33] *Ibid.*, XIII, No. 3569, p. 268, Eulenburg to Foreign Office, July 6, 1899.

[34] *Ibid.*, XIII, No. 3571, p. 269, Kaiser to Münster, July 16, 1899; No. 3581, p. 280, Münster to Foreign Office, August 18, 1899.

purposed to keep open the question of Alsace-Lorraine. And, with a very scrupulous caution, he feared
that if France's rival were once settled with, there
would be no holding France at all.[35] A few weeks later
he told the Russian ambassador (May 5) that there
was one condition upon which Germany would con-
clude any agreement or alliance with Russia—as with
Russia and France together—namely, that Russia
and France would declare themselves ready to mutually guarantee the present territories of the three powers. Future co-operation between France and Germany, he said, was not impossible; but it must depend
upon an acknowledgment of the Peace of Frankfort.
Considering French aspirations of revenge, however,
Germany could not engage herself against England.[36]
Neither were they, for that matter, very sanguine in
Russia. The newspaper *Swet* pointed out that all serious endeavors in Paris to bring about a Franco-German reconciliation were under the impulse of the colonial faction, and rested notoriously upon motives of
hostility toward England. But having now lost Fashoda, France had little to gain after the event by a
tardy reconciliation with Germany.[37]

It was the spirit and policy of *revanche*, therefore,
which now as before stood in the way of Franco-Ger-

[35] *Ibid.*, XIII, No. 3566, p. 264, memorandum by Bülow,
March 14, 1899.

[36] *Ibid.*, XIII, No. 3567, p. 266, memorandum by Bülow, May
5, 1899 (cf. *ibid.*, XIV, Nos. 4016, 4019).

[37] *Ibid.*, XIII, No. 3583, p. 282, Radolin to Hohenlohe, October 6, 1899.

man reconciliation. Upon the question of the Peace of Frankfort Germany was not to be moved. Even in the matter of the passport system in Alsace-Lorraine, the German military authorities would permit no relaxation, not, they admitted, out of fear of French espionage, but lest France should be encouraged to hope for the recovery of the Reichsland.[38]

Also, as before, the Russian Alliance was shown to be of small avail in shielding France from the consequences of *revanche*. The Fashoda incident had been a sharp lesson to France in the uses of the Russian alliance. England had not feared it, but worse still, Germany had learned that there was no fight in it. And now after Fashoda Russia was still on suspiciously good terms with Germany. Had France known all, it is possible that she would have been not less disturbed. In Berlin and St. Petersburg during the summer there were discussions of a possible *rapprochement*, in which while the Germans, on one side, held steadily to the contention that there could be no intimacy so long as Russia persisted in the French alliance, the Russians, on the other, gave repeated assurances that the alliance did not imply aggression against Germany—that in spite of the *entente assez intime*, Russia was anxious for the closest relations with Germany.[39] And as before, Russia represented herself as a sort of condescending patron of France, an *ehrlicher Makler*, inter-

[38] *Ibid.,* XIII, No. 3562, p. 257, Bülow to Münster, February 9, 1899.

[39] *Ibid.,* XIV, No. 4017, p. 538, memorandum by Bülow, April 18, 1899.

preting France to Europe and vouching for the honesty of French intentions. This was shady conduct in an ally; and the alliance was plainly growing much too loose and tenuous. In August Delcassé undertook a journey to St. Petersburg to reknit, if possible, the shaken fabric of Franco-Russian relations. The particular object of his errand was to persuade the Czar to extend the application of the military convention of 1893–94. That convention had been explicitly limited in duration; it was to stand only so long as the Triple Alliance lasted.[40] But what if the Triple Alliance should be dissolved by the collapse of one of its members? of Austria, for instance? Delcassé had conceived a dread of that very eventuality; and he now explained his fears to the Czar, who showed himself willing to join in averting the lapse of the convention.[41] Accordingly, there was an exchange of notes between Delcassé and Muravieff committing the alliance not only, as before, to the maintenance of "peace" but also and expressly to the maintenance of the "balance of power"; and affirming that the military convention of 1893–94 should remain in force as long as the prior diplomatic agreement upon which it rested.[42] It was a timely effort; but at the moment an impenetrable mystery hid both the object and the success of Delcassé's mission. The conviction continued to grow,

[40] *Documents Diplomatiques: L'all. franco-russe,* No. 71, p. 92, text.

[41] *Ibid.,* No. 95, pp. 131–32, Delcassé to Loubet, August 12, 1899.

[42] *Ibid.,* Nos. 93 and 94, pp. 129–30, August 9, 1899.

therefore, among French politicians and among the masses through the press, that France had been duped by Russia.[43] And when in November the Czar visited Potsdam, French suspicions were only further excited.[44]

Here, then, were reasons enough for French discontent with the European situation: Germany unpropitiated, Russia lukewarm, and Great Britain openly hostile and triumphant. The unnatural union of those ill-assorted policies, *revanche* and colonies, was bringing forth an evil brood of mixed purposes, diffused efforts, and in a crisis wavering and weakness. At least one colonial adventure had but lately proved a total loss, and *revanche* remained a liability only partially eased by the Russian alliance. The brief and belated move toward a reconciliation with Germany in the winter of 1898–99 was a false step and soon retracted. For not only would a practical and positive reconciliation have belied the deepest French instincts but it would also have come too late to reverse the Fashoda defeat. There was no object now in renouncing *revanche* since it had already exacted its price in colonies.

But with *revanche* remaining as the perennial circumstance of existence, what then was to become of colonial expansion? The time had been when it was the habit in Europe to regard colonial questions as only

[43] *G.P.*, XIII, No. 3577, p. 274, Münster to Hohenlohe, August 7, 1899.

[44] *Ibid.*, XIII, No. 3585, p. 283, Münster to Hohenlohe, November 10, 1899.

accessory to the main European issues. Indeed, it was for the first time in history that in 1884 a Conference of Powers had been called at Berlin to discuss matters which did not directly touch Europe. But little by little colonies had come to dominate European politics; and the *Weltpolitik* of the nineties was not quite the same as *la grande politique* of an earlier day. To France, especially, her colonies were very dear. Was she, then, to be cheated of her prospects in Africa by the German menace in Europe?

It must have occurred to many Frenchmen even before the lamentable events of 1898 that the awkward dilemma between *revanche* and colonies might possibly be evaded by an understanding with England. Thereby they would gain at once an added buttress against Germany, and a new liberty of expansion as well. Security in both directions would spring from the single arrangement. It was very like a fusion of the two conflicting objects of their policy—one policy compounded out of two. The Russian alliance had had no such happy magical power.

There may, of course, have been some apprehension that the Russian alliance would itself prove an obstacle to a French *rapprochement* with Great Britain. It seems that Baron Holstein was of that opinion. Writing in April of 1899, and reasoning as usual with some parade of subtlety and statecraft, he declared that France could not be reconciled to England; that one of England's first demands would be that France abandon Russia; and that it was absurd to suppose that England could buy off Russia by the concessions and compensations which she might offer France in Africa.[45] It will be remembered, however, that the Russian court and especially the two empresses had Anglophil leanings. Moreover, in April, 1899, the two powers had composed their differences in China by an exchange of notes, whereby the territories north of the Great Wall were to be left to Russian penetration and the Yangtze Basin to British.[46] And in June Mura-vieff had actually threatened the Germans with an Anglo-Russian accord in the Near East if Germany declined any accommodation. He told the German ambassador that it was an error to suppose that England was an implacable rival of Russia.[47]

The Fashoda crisis seemed, therefore, to present Delcassé with two alternatives of policy toward Great Britain. He could have stuck to his position and his arguments and adjourned a settlement with Great Britain to a more favorable opportunity. That was the course taken under similar circumstances by Du-clere sixteen years before in Egypt; and France had gained nothing by persisting in it. Or Delcassé could have entered upon a process of liquidation of all issues between France and England beginning with Fashoda, and as the sequel has shown, he would have eventually

[45] *Ibid.*, XIV, No. 4016, p. 536, memorandum by Holstein, April 17, 1899; Eckardstein, *op. cit.*, pp. 128–29.

[46] *British Documents,* I, No. 61, p. 40, Salisbury to Bax-Iron-side, April 30, 1899.

[47] *G.P.*, XIV, No. 4022, p. 551, Radolin to Hohenlohe, June 29, 1899.

shifted the prodigious weights in the balance of Europe.

Both France and Great Britain, therefore, were ripe for conversion to new practices and doctrines; the accepted diplomatic rubrics were losing their sanction, and a vain repetition of the old formulas was bringing no consolation. It began to appear that the double-ended policy of colonies and *revanche* could be safely carried out in France only with the indulgence of Great Britain; and that Great Britain could break her long isolation only by conciliating France. What, then, were the chances of compassing such indulgence and such conciliation? De Courcel had said to Salisbury (October 5, 1898), "Qui sait si, à la suite d'un accord réglant la difficulté présente, le long malentendu crée entre la France et l'Angleterre ne se trouverait pas implicitement dissipé au grand avantage des deux pays?"[48] Was he simply emitting one of the platitudinous and pious hopes common enough in the usages of diplomacy, or did his words really have in them some strain of candor and of genuine desire and reasoned expectation? And would Chamberlain (Bismarck's *wilder Junge*) now execute his threats against Germany[49] and actually carry through a *rapprochement* toward France and perhaps toward Russia too?

It was fortunate that in both France and England new men were coming to power, or had already come to power, who began to work more or less consciously

[48] *Documents Diplomatiques: Haut Nil,* No. 25, De Courcel to Delcassé, October 5, 1898.

[49] *Cambridge History of British Foreign Policy,* III, 615.

toward a better Anglo-French understanding. Lord Salisbury, with his well-known German leanings, was soon to be replaced at the Foreign Office by Lord Lansdowne, a French scholar and with French blood running in his veins.[50] The Prince of Wales, who was personally well liked in France, lavished his urbanity and charm of manners to exorcise French national antipathy; indeed, after his accession he came to be regarded as almost the initiator of the entente.[51] Baron de Courcel, one-time ambassador to Germany and French delegate to the African Conference at Berlin, where he had been much in opposition to Great Britain,[52] was recalled from London during the winter of 1898. His post was filled by M. Paul Cambon, a patient disseminator of good will.[53] Above all there was M. Delcassé, the same who had withstood Lord Salisbury so manfully over Fashoda, but who was shortly to become chief advocate of the policy of an entente between France and England.

Delcassé had become foreign minister in that very summer of 1898, and the disagreeable experiences of his first months in office may well have confirmed him in the opinion that France could not go on forever at enmity with Great Britain. When in June, 1899, the Socialists first got a footing in the government, domestic policies were pushed to the front, leaving Del-

[50] *Ibid.,* III, 615.

[51] Tardieu, *France and the Alliances,* p. 60.

[52] Schefer, *D'une guerre à l'autre,* p. 113.

[53] *British Documents,* I, 191, p. 165, Monson to Salisbury, September 18, 1898.

cassé the greater liberty in foreign affairs. He soon won a position of eminence and power in both the Foreign Office and the Chambre as assured as had been that of Hanotaux before him, and he fully disproved the old jibe that he was "étranger aux affaires."[54] He remained continuously in office through a half-dozen changes of ministry, and was not turned out until his schemes had taken substance in a convention with Great Britain, and he himself had won the distinction of being specially marked out for disfavor by the Imperial German government. Delcassé was not, indeed, the first nor the only Frenchman in office to contemplate making friends with England. In the spring of 1899 there were other members of the Dupuy ministry who leaned that way, as did also President Faure himself. And even in the earlier Méline ministry, in which Hanotaux had been Foreign Minister, certain members of government were disposed toward conciliation.[55] But it was Delcassé who was destined to bring the new policy to its happy conclusion.

It is possible that the diplomatic revolution which was already coming fairly into view before the turn of the century would have run its course without the aid of a Fashoda incident. Perhaps other influences and events, some of which have already been touched upon, would have driven it along with sufficient force to bring it to fulfilment. And it is presumable, at least, that so momentous a change could not have sprung

[54] *G.P.*, XIII, No. 3644, p. 340, Münster to Hohenlohe, December 4, 1899.

[55] Schefer, *op. cit.*, pp. 232 ff.

from a single impulse, however prepotent. But on examination it seems that the Fashoda incident did in reality contribute something from its own proper energy toward the advent of a new situation in Europe; that the ground so torn and furrowed by the Fashoda controversy became in a special sense the fruitful seed-bed of the Anglo-French entente.

The conventions of the 8th of April, 1904, which were the symbol and expression of the new entente, did not deal with general formulas of alliance but with particular expedients for composing outstanding differences. They were compacts made up of practical provisions for terminating specific discords. Now chief among the matters of disagreement there expressly treated was Egypt; and it is demonstrable that a settlement in Egypt was rendered immeasurably easier by the prior settlement touching the upper Nile.

The French rancor against Great Britain in Egypt had for more than fifteen years fretted itself in hourly expectation of seeing Great Britain turned out. When in 1882 England intervened alone it was not by resolution or conviction but by hesitancies and half-measures. The bombardment of Alexandria bore the aspect of a random impulse of the Gladstone government; and to Bright it seemed that the situation had simply been "handed over to the ruffians of the fleet."[56]

As Great Britain began, so it continued in a policy of drifting and piously hoping for the best; and par-

[56] Trevelyan: *The Life of John Bright*, p. 435.

ticularly it elected to believe against plain evidence to the contrary that it was not irrevocably committed in Egypt. Almost at once after the battle of Tel-el-Kebir the British government gave a contingent promise of early evacuation.[57] It was beyond question their sincere intention, and they seem to have been anxious to have all Europe believe it so. Early in 1883 Lord Dufferin, under instructions, outlined a scheme for independent and constitutional government to be set up in Egypt against the approaching day of British departure.[58] Sir E. Baring was confident (1883) that if he could have two thousand men and a free hand to settle the affairs of the Khedive, in twelve months "there shall not be a British soldier in Egypt."[59] In 1887 the Wolff Convention, negotiated with Turkey, contemplated an evacuation within three years. In 1894 Sir Thomas Barclay was warned by friends not to accept an Egyptian judgeship, owing to the possibility of evacuation.[60] And even as late as March, 1898, when a question arose in Parliament of building barracks for British troops in Egypt, there were protests against charging the British treasury with the expense on the ground that "apparently we are only lodgers in Egypt."[61] Thus England was herself chiefly

[57] *British and Foreign State Papers,* LXXV (1883–84), 676: Granville to Her Majesty's representatives in Paris, Berlin, Vienna, and St. Petersburg, January 3, 1883.

[58] Wallace, *Egypt and Egyptian Question,* pp. 430 ff.

[59] Cromer, *Modern Egypt,* II, 359.

[60] Barclay, *Thirty Years Anglo-French Reminiscences,* p. 113.

[61] *Parliamentary Debates,* LV, 932, General Russell.

responsible for keeping alive the idea and expectation of an imminent withdrawal. And since it was largely upon these deferred hopes that French jealousy sustained itself, it should have been possible to abate the jealousy by quenching the hopes.

But to have now permitted France to retain a foothold on the upper Nile would have been to raise again French anticipations in Egypt. It was so that the French themselves understood the situation. Carnot had said to Monteil: "Je veux rouvrir la question d'Égypte."[62] After the encounter at Fashoda the *Journal* of Paris was quoted as contending that "the retirement of France from Fashoda would imply the recognition of the seizure of Egypt and the abandonment of our African policy."[63] Bonvalot declared (September 30) that "the occupation of Fashoda by Marchand is the crucial affair. It is the keystone of the settlement of the Delta question and the English occupation."[64] And Monson reported from Paris that the French government "see clearly enough that the recent operations have simply clinched our hold upon Egypt more tightly, and that British 'practice' cannot be assimilated to French 'logic.' "[65]

There is authoritative and even more explicit evidence that the conscious object of the French govern-

[62] Velay, *Les rivalités franco-anglaises en Egypte, 1876–1904,* p. 163.

[63] *London Times,* September 21.

[64] *Ibid.,* September 30.

[65] *British Documents,* I, No. 188, p. 164, Monson to Salisbury, September 8, 1898.

ment in sanctioning the Marchand mission had been to raise again the Egyptian question. The expedition was commissioned in the usual way by the Minister of the Colonies. But its chief sponsor and real author was the Minister of Foreign Affairs, M. Hanotaux. And it is Hanotaux himself who has explained that the Marchand mission was designed as a stratagem in diplomacy rather than as an enterprise of expansion. The purpose was not primarily to conquer or annex territory, nor to secure economic outlets, nor even to win some conspicuous advantage which might serve French diplomacy as material for negotiation. Rather the expedition replaced negotiation—"C'etait la négociation elle-même."[66] Great Britain had long and obstinately refused to allow herself to be called to account in Egypt. The intent of the French government was, therefore, to reopen the Egyptian question by a back door through the Sudan. To thwart British designs in the Sudan in whatever way would, it was hoped, force a discussion implicit or explicit of England's position in Egypt. If England could only be goaded into making a defense by argument, she would be virtually admitting that she was answerable to Europe as represented in France. In Hanotaux' own words, "Pour l'Angleterre, consentir à discuter, c'est se limiter."[67]

That the Fashoda question very intimately touched the older Egyptian question in the minds of Frenchmen is further shown by the conduct of the French government during the Fashoda negotiations.

[66] Hanotaux, *Fachoda,* p. 137.

[67] *Ibid.,* p. 88.

De Courcel said to Salisbury (October 5) that when Hanotaux had recognized the rights of Egypt and the Sultan in the upper Nile, when also he had admitted that some day the lost provinces might be legitimately reclaimed for Egypt, his declarations pointedly implied that when the ultimate fate of the Sudan should fall to be considered, the examination would necessarily reopen the whole Egyptian question. De Courcel asserted, moreover, that he was persuaded that M. Delcassé would not shrink from such a controversy, even though he might not share all of Hanotaux' ideas on the value of the claims advanced in the name of Egypt.[68]

Later on, however, it began to appear that it might have been after all an error to raise the Egyptian question if it were not to be settled in favor of France. It would have been fairly easy to demonstrate in argument that Great Britain's position in Egypt was a political solecism, but it was notorious that incongruities of theory held no terrors for the British mind. England's occupation of Egypt was unconventional, no doubt; but the point was to get her turned out, and simply to convict her of irregularity would not of itself accomplish that end. Delcassé may also have reflected that if England were forced to find some formula to cover the anomaly of her status in Egypt, she might propound one so uncompromising to French claims that France would have got nothing out of it except perhaps a mild gratification of her taste for the

[68] *Documents Diplomatiques: Haut Nil,* No. 25, De Courcel to Delcassé, October 5, 1898.

logical proprieties. When, therefore, the French case
in the Sudan seemed to be definitely lost, and the negotiations were nearing a conclusion, Delcassé manifest-
ed a fear that the questions of the Bahr-el-Ghazelle
and of Egypt might be involved together in a double
disaster, and he was at great pains to dissociate, if
possible, the one from the other. Cambon, the new ambassador in London, was led therefore to object to
some of Salisbury's proposals on the express grounds
that they would raise implicitly the Egyptian question.[69] And Delcassé wrote to the ambassador that it
was to avoid that very hazard that from the first he
had wished to incorporate the Bahr-el-Ghazelle agreement as an additional declaration in the Anglo-French
convention of the previous June, that is to say, in an
instrument dealing with west and central African territories. Thereby he hoped to avoid the appearance of
having been peremptorily excluded from the Nile; the
delimitation toward the Nile could now, he thought, be
looked upon as properly a continuation of the delimitation of the French Niger possessions.[70] Delcassé insisted on expurgating from the first drafts of the declaration any least mention of the Egyptian question.
He was even careful to strike out the words "Ce qui
était en 1882 la province égyptienne de Darfour," and
had it read instead, "Ce qui était en 1882 la province
de Darfour."[71]

[69] *Ibid.: Correspondance concernant la déclaration additionelle du 21 Mars, 1899,* No. 10, Cambon to Delcassé, March 2, 1899.

[70] *Ibid.,* Nos. 6, 11, Delcassé to Cambon, March 7, 1899.

[71] *Ibid.,* Nos. 15–16, March 20, 1899.

But just as Hanotaux had failed to force a discussion of the Egyptian question, so Delcassé failed to keep it from being brought to a decision without discussion. All his precautions did not prevent French pretensions in Egypt from falling into a like condemnation with her pretensions in the Sudan. The main proposition and its corollary suffered refutation together. Even the exclusion of the Egyptian government from participation in the final partition agreement, and the omission of the very name of Egypt from the terms of the convention were but a tacit acknowledgment of Great Britain's sole competence in the Nile Valley.

Therefore, in dealing so uncompromisingly with the French over Fashoda, the British had at last nerved themselves to do what they should have done long before, that is, avow their intention of remaining indefinitely in the Nile Valley. Their legal status was not yet altered in Egypt proper. The old trouble-making shifts and pretexts and fictions remained. New ones were invented for the Sudan and solemnly set forth in the Anglo-Egyptian Agreement of January 19, 1899—that "hybrid form of government, hitherto unknown to international jurisprudence,"[72] which in these latter days is bringing forth its own crop of heartburnings. But the real position of Great Britain in Egypt was not thenceforward doubtful, even though the diplomatic euphemisms were still conscientiously employed. The Fashoda incident demonstrated

[72] Cromer, *Modern Egypt,* II, 115.

that England was not to be expelled from Egypt except by war, and, knowing that, the French learned resignation.

The German Emperor was reported to have said that the battle of Omderman was of no less importance than the battle of Waterloo.[73] Doubtless he made too much of the issues in the Sudan; and, besides, Kitchener's victory did not mark the termination of the crisis, but was rather its proximate cause. But at least in the Fashoda settlement the long and bitter era of African rivalry between Great Britain and France ended with this last definitive award of a territorial prize. New matters of contention would no doubt have arisen; but in that moment of truce national sentiments were fortunately diverted from the old evil rut of chronic enmity. The Transvaal almost immediately drew off Great Britain's attention southward in Africa; and Delcassé, not being of a vengeful turn, refrained from making any capital whatever out of Britain's embarrassments. Moreover, France, having accepted with fortitude her check in the Sudan, now turned to Morocco and began a more serious pursuit of her interests in the west. As it turned out, it was in Morocco that she was to find her true compensation for reverses on the Nile. The essence of the conventions of 1904, so far as they touched Africa, was a balance of Morocco against Egypt.

Even after 1904 France did not cease to interest herself regretfully in Egypt, though certainly without the passionate repinings of the days before Fashoda.

[73] *Parliamentary Debates,* LXVII, 488, February 24, 1899.

There remained a hope, conscientiously repressed, that a time would come when Egypt would cease to be under British domination. De Freycinet even speculated rather wistfully on the possibility that England might yet be moved to evacuate Egypt if by keeping the Sudan she could secure the route to India.[74] It was a suggestion which may prove to have been prophetic. However that may be, since 1904 France has loyally refrained from interference in the Nile Valley. There remains an Egyptian question to this day, but it has quite changed its face and is no more a controversy between European powers but between Great Britain and the Egyptian nation. While the conventions of 1904 were still new, a Frenchman remarked of them, "Il faut bien avouer que les précédents ne sont guère encourageants"; in 1830, 1840, and 1898 "on fut à deux doigts d'une rupture."[75] Nevertheless, events were propitious for the new-made entente. Fashoda was forgotten; the very name of the place was changed. And in less than seven years after Marchand had confronted Kitchener all Europe knew that in Africa France and Great Britain were virtually allies.

[74] De Freycinet, *La question d'Égypte,* pp. 442 ff.

[75] Darcy, *France et Angleterre,* p. 6.

WORKS CITED

WORKS CITED

SOURCES

FRANCE

Documents Diplomatiques.
> *Convention du 14 juin, 1898.*
> *Affaires du Haut Nil et du Bahr-el-Ghazal, 1897–8.*
> *Correspondance concernant la déclaration additionelle du 21 Mars, 1899.*
> *L'alliance franco-russe.*
Archives Diplomatiques, Vols. I–II.
Journal officiel, Documents parlementaires, Chambre.

GERMANY

Die Grosse Politik der Europäischen Kabinette, 1871–1914. Vols. XIII and XIV.

GREAT BRITAIN

British and Foreign State Papers. Vol. LXXV, 1883–84; Vol. XC, 1897–98; Vol. XCI, 1898–99.
Parliamentary Papers.
> *Egypt Nos. 2 and 3, 1898.*
> *Egypt Nos. 2 and 4, 1899.*
> *Egypt No. 2, 1901.*
> *Egypt No. 2, 1904.*
Parliamentary Debates.
> Hansard, Vols. LX, LXVII–LXVIII.
British Documents on the Origins of the War, 1898–1914. Vol. I. *The End of British Isolation.*
The Kaiser's Letters to the Tsar. Edited by N. F. Grant. London, 1920.
PRIBRAM, ALFRED FRANZIS. *The Secret Treaties of Austria-Hungary, 1879–1914.* Edited by A. C. Coolidge. Harvard University Press, 1920.

SECONDARY AUTHORITIES

BAKER, S. W. *The Albert Nyanza.* London, 1866. *Ismailia.* London, 1874.

BARCLAY, SIR THOMAS. *Thirty Years Anglo-French Reminiscences.* New York, 1914.

BÜLOW, PRINCE VON. *Imperial Germany.* English translation by M. A. Lewenz. New York, 1917.

Cambridge History of British Foreign Policy. Edited by Sir A. W. Ward and G. P. Gooch. New York, 1922.

CAMERON, D. A. *Egypt in the Nineteenth Century.* London, 1898.

CHURCHILL, W. S. *The River War.* Edited by Colonel F. Rhodes. London.

CRISPI, FRANCESCO. *Memoirs, 1819–1901.* English translation by Mary Prichard-Agnetti. London, 1914.

CROMER, EARL OF. *Modern Egypt.* London, 1908.

DARCY, J. *France et Angleterre: Cent années de rivalité colonial.* Paris, 1904.

DICKINSON, G. LOWES. *The International Anarchy, 1904–1914.* New York, 1926.

EARLE, EDWARD MEAD. *Turkey, the Great Powers, and the Bagdad Railway.* New York, 1923.

ECKARDSTEIN, BARON VON. *Ten Years at the Court of St. James.* Translated by George Young. London, 1921.

DE FREYCINET, C. L. *La question d'Égypte.* Paris, 1905.

FULLERTON, W. MORTON. *Problems of Power.* London, 1914.

GLEICHEN, LIEUTENANT COLONEL, COUNT (Editor). *The Anglo-Egyptian Sudan.* Compendium prepared by officers of the Sudan government. London, 1905.

GOOCH, G. P. *History of Modern Europe, 1878–1919.* New York, 1922.

GORDON, MAJ. GEN. C. G. *Journals at Khartoum.* Edited by Egmont Hake. London, 1885.

GREY, VISCOUNT. *Twenty-five Years.* New York, 1925.

GWYNN, S. L., AND TUCKWELL, G. M. *The Life of the Rt. Hon. Sir Charles W. Dilke.* New York, 1917.

HAMANN, OTTO. *The World Policy of Germany, 1890–1912.* English translation by Maude A. Huttman. New York, 1927.

HANOTAUX, GABRIEL. *Fachoda.* Paris, 1909.

HARRIS, NORMAN DWIGHT. *Europe and Africa.* New York, 1926.

HOHENLOHE-SCHILLINGSFUERST, PRINCE CHLODWIG. *Memoirs.* English edition by G. W. Chrystal. New York, 1906.

INTELLIGENCE SECRETARY, SUDAN AGENCY. *Sudan Almanac, 1923.* London.

The Kaiser's Memoirs, 1888–1918. Translated by T. R. Ybarra. New York, 1922.

LEE, SIR SIDNEY. *King Edward VII.* New York, 1925.

MÉVIL, ANDRÉ. *De la paix de Francfort à la conférence d'Algésiras.* Paris, 1909.

MORLEY, JOHN. *The Life of William Ewart Gladstone.* New York, 1911.

MAURRAS, CHARLES. *Quand les Francais ne s'aimaient pas.* Paris, 1916.

NEUFELD, CHARLES. *A Prisoner of the Khalifa.* London, 1899.

RODD, SIR J. RENNEL. *Social and Diplomatic Memories.* Second Series, *1894–1901.* London, 1923.

ROSE, J. H. *The Development of the European Nations, 1870–1900.* New York, 1905.

ROUARD DE CARD, E. *Les territoires africains et les conventions franco-anglaises.* Paris, 1901.

SCHEFER, CHRISTIAN. *D'une guerre à l'autre.* Paris, 1920.

SEYMOUR, CHARLES. *The Diplomatic Background of the War, 1870–1914.* New Haven, 1916.

STANLEY, H. M. *Slavery and the Slave Trade.* New York, 1893.

STEEVENS, G. W. *With Kitchener to Khartoum.* New York, 1899.

STUART, GRAHAM H. *French Foreign Policy*. New York, 1921.

TARDIEU, ANDRÉ. *France and the Alliances*. New York, 1908.

TREVELYAN, G. M. *The Life of John Bright*. London, 1913.

VELAY, E. *Les rivalités franco-anglaises en Egypte, 1876–1904*. Nîmes, 1904.

WALLACE, D. MACKENZIE. *Egypt and the Egyptian Question*. London, 1883.

WHITE, A. SILVA. *The Expansion of Egypt*. London, 1899.

PERIODICALS

ALDEN, W. L. "Erythrea," *Contemporary Review*, Vol. LXXI (January, 1897).

ANONYMOUS. "France, Russia and the Nile," *Cont. Rev.*, Vol. LXXIV (December, 1898).

CHURCHILL, W. S. "The Fashoda Incident," *North American Review*, CLXVII, 736.

DECLE, LIONEL. "The Fashoda Question," *Fortnightly Review*, Vol. LXIV (November, 1898).

DEHERAIN, HENRI. "La succession de l'Égypte dans la province Équatoriale," *Revue des deux mondes*, May, 1894, p. 312.

DIPLOMATICUS. "Fashoda and Lord Salisbury's Vindication," *Fortnightly Review*, Vol. LXIV (December, 1898).

FERRY, RENÉ. "L'Éthiopie et l'expansion européenne en Afrique orientale," *Annales des sciences politiques*, XXV, 17.

LEBON, A. "La mission Marchand et le cabinet Méline," *Revue des deux mondes*, March, 1900.

MOUREY, CHARLES. "De l'Atlantique au Nil," *Annales des sciences politiques*, XIV, 43.

PASQUET, D. "Comment la France a perdu l'Egypte," *Revue historique,* CVI, 27–59.

SCHMITT, B. E. "Triple Alliance and Triple Entente," *American Historical Review,* Vol. XXIX (April, 1927).

London Times.

INDEX

INDEX